An Agency of Their Own

Sex Worker Union Organizing

An Agency of Their Own

Sex Worker Union Organizing

Gregor Gall

Winchester, UK
Washington, USA

First published by Zero Books, 2012
Zero Books is an imprint of John Hunt Publishing Ltd., Laurel House, Station Approach,
Alresford, Hants, SO24 9JH, UK
office1@jhpbooks.net
www.johnhuntpublishing.com

For distributor details and how to order please visit the 'Ordering' section on our website.

A CIP catalogue record for this book is available from the British Library.

Design: Stuart Davies

Printed and bound by CPI Group (UK) Ltd, Croydon, CR0 4YY

We operate a distinctive and ethical publishing philosophy in all
areas of our business, from our global network of authors to
production and worldwide distribution.

CONTENTS

Dedicated to my parents, Alisan and Jim,
for all their kindness and support down the years.

Introduction

Sex work – especially prostitution – is often described as 'the world's oldest profession', even by sex workers and their advocates. But if sex work was a profession, never mind the oldest one, then sex workers would not feel compelled to collectively organize themselves as they have done in order to fight for their rights. This is because professions, like law and medicine, not only control entry into their own ranks and internally regulate themselves – making themselves into powerful collectives – but they are also accorded large measures of respect and worth by society in general.[1]

None of this is true so far for sex workers. Consequently, they have organized themselves into collectives to fight for themselves and their interests. In other words, and as the title of this book makes clear, sex workers have fought to establish their own collective *agency* in order to exert control over and to begin determining their working lives as well as their lives in general. Many have attempted to do so through creating their own labor unions or by joining existing labor unions. This book not only tells the story of how they have done so but analyzes what success they have had so far and what barriers and obstacles they face in making their unions more effective.

There is something both inherently interesting and challenging in the matter of sex workers unionizing. Interesting in that it is not often heard of and seems counter-intuitive given that sex workers are seldom employees: challenging in that selling sex and sexual services are seen by many as morally and politically repugnant and because sex workers are not employed making unionization innately difficult. But sex workers have been attempting to unionize themselves for well over twenty years now. This increases the importance of this book examining those efforts, looking at the where, why, when and how of their story as well as the successes and difficulties faced in doing so.

To intellectually and practically contemplate both sex workers unionizing themselves and unions unionizing sex workers, several foundations are necessary. The first is the existence of the perspective that 'sex work' is a legitimate form of employment and economic activity and as such requires unionization to reduce the exploitation and oppression of sex workers associated with it. The second is the related perspective that sex workers perform sexual labor comprised of emotional, erotic and manual or physical labors which are but variants of what may be termed conventional wage labor, and in particular 'emotional' labor performed by a variety of other service workers. Third is evidence of a political awakening in the consciousness of those who are usually regarded as quintessentially downtrodden and super-exploited women, who are often regarded as either victims or unchaste. Fourth is that the sex industry represents a large and growing form of economic activity, comprising a diverse and heterogeneous array of activities ranging from prostitutes, escorts, and massage parlor workers, to strippers/exotic dancers/lapdancers, pornographic models, pornographic actors/actresses, and sex chatline telephone and text operators. This relatively hidden industry involves hundreds of thousands of workers in economic activity. The rest of this chapter briefly expands on these themes and introduces some others in relation to unionization in order to understand the ideas and premises behind sex worker unionization.

Sex as work

The key foundation for organizing sex workers is the perspective of viewing sex workers as workers who have nothing to sell to survive economically but their labor. This labor is deemed to be of a) sufficient level of moral legitimacy and b) social worth as a form of employment to be comparable to other forms of labor and paid employment that are deemed worthy and acceptable to organize. The perspective is also of sex workers selling sexual services and not their bodies and persons *per se*.[2] A distinction is not especially made between acts which involve selling of sex and selling sexual stimulation, or between those acts which involve entering a body, acting on another body or entering personal spaces and those which involve the production of such imagery. Allied to this, sex work is viewed as comprising work that *can be* socially useful and *can* provide job satisfaction, personal fulfilment, empowerment and self-actualization, where becoming a sex worker *can be* a genuine life choice. The conditions of this potentiality are acknowledged to exist to some extent in the present and to be greatly enhanced in the future under different conditions, namely, of sex worker control. However, it is recognized that alongside these potential benefits, there are downsides in terms of violence, stigmatization, poor pay and conditions of employment, and job and employment insecurity. These downsides are believed to exist as much from the way in which society and the state view and regulate sex work as they are about the selling of sex and sexual services under capitalism. In short and put altogether, this is the 'sex work' discourse.

This discourse emerged from the 1970s onwards and in response to two immediate stimuli, namely, an attempt to deal more efficiently and effectively with the immediate challenges facing prostitutes (of stigma, harassment and violence) and to respond to the 'prostitution as rape, misogyny and male power' discourse of the radical feminists. At the core of the sex work discourse is a view that the abolition of sex work in the short- to medium- term is neither possible nor desirable. Consequently, reform and changes in law, regulation and social values are believed to present more attainable goals (in the vein of unions attempting to better the terms of the wage-effort bargain rather than abolish wage labor). To flesh out the aforementioned basic exposition, the sex work discourse can defined as comprising the following beliefs, assumptions and propositions:

- The production and exchange – routinely called 'selling' – of sex, sexual services and sexual artefacts are a means of economic subsistence or income for the wage-laborers that carry them out and represent the selling of wage labor, regardless of variations in the real or formal employment relationship contained therein.

- The 'selling' of sex, sexual services and sexual artefacts represents one of the main aspects of the commodification of sex under capitalism or the 'free market'. The 'selling' represents the transformation of labor into an exchange value, and the labor involved in addition to any physical labor, is primarily of an emotional and psychological nature because of the direct interaction with the consumer where a marketable persona is constructed which represents an alienation or estrangement from the inherent self, creating dissonance. Consequently, the labor is denoted as 'erotic' labor and can be subsumed with the category of 'service work'.

- Sex work – the labor involved in generating sex, sexual services and sexual artefacts – is not solely the result of economic or physical compulsion and coercion but also of choice, albeit of a narrowed nature; that is, a situation where choice is compelled to be taken from a limited range of options determined by other social forces. Lack of choice represents an environment of both inequality of opportunity and outcome, compelling personal and individual decisions for constructing one's own life chances. Where sex work is coerced by a third party, particularly through trafficking, this should be recognized as such but without

4

negating the existence of (voluntary) migrant sex workers.

- Sex work represents a rational choice and action given limitations on work and employment opportunities for sex workers. Its abolition would deny sex workers a means of subsistence and sustaining themselves and their dependents.

- Sex work is not uniform, monolithic or universal in its form, content and environment. Rather, it does, and can, portray a range of varying micro- or meso-level characteristics within the framework set out above.

- Sex work *can* offer benefits *vis-à-vis* remuneration and working conditions (hours, autonomy, self-direction, job satisfaction which may or may not include some sexual pleasure and gratification) which are superior to many jobs available to those without much in the way of skills, qualification and job experience as well as superior to living on state benefits. Performing and carrying out sex work requires certain social and interpersonal skills.

- Many of the problems associated with sex work for sex workers relate to stigmatization, criminalization and discrimination and the subsequent marginalization and social exclusion (in addition to any legal discrimination or neglect) of sex workers. Illegality and criminalization in addition to their direct punitive measures also perpetuate stigmatization. These characteristics can be tackled and ameliorated in the here and now by an array of measures. Moreover, the realization and/or further realization of what are held to be satisfying aspects of sex work can be achieved by regulation (self- and extra-self) and the demeaning, damaging and degrading aspects can also be lessened by the same means.

- Sex workers need concrete rights in the here and now and these are better concerned with being grounded in immediate economic and power relations; this is often and mainly achieved through legal reform such as decriminalization or legalization of sex work. Where sex work is decriminalized or legal, sex workers require and are entitled to rights of workers (human, labor, and economic) to prevent non-payment of wages, unfair dismissal, victimization and the like.

- Sex work and sex workers are regulated by bureaucratic and social structures and social discourse in the same way as conventional work. As sex work is work, the industry should be regulated as such, on a par with other business sectors, thus paying far less attention to morality, criminality, policing and so on.

- Sex work involves negotiation by sex workers with employers, facilitators or operators (e.g. club owners) and customers, providing potential leverage points by individual and collective means for improving remuneration and working conditions.

- Sex workers, as workers, manufacture identities and strategies for attempting to exercise control over effort, remuneration, safety, trauma and the like in the same way that other workers do. Sex workers also require certain skills to do their jobs effectively, either for their own or their employers' interests, *vis-à-vis* various social skills such as 'deep' and 'surface' acting. In this regard, dissociation is viewed not as a negative, but rather as a positive. Such dissociation is possible because it is not the body that is sold but sexual services, even though these services are intimately attached to body.

- It is inconsistent, illogical and harmful to argue, and operationalize, the position of 'for sex workers, against sex work' because sex work and sex workers are not products of capitalism and/or patriarchy *per se* and they can exist under different, better and future social relations.

6

From Civil to Worker Rights and from Pressure Groups to Labor Unionism

The transition in thought and organization amongst sex workers from focussing upon civil and political rights to economic, worker and union rights, and from pressure group activity to union organizing, constitute two critical and closely related developments to the emergence of the sex work discourse. The initial groups of sex workers (i.e. prostitutes who were often aided by non-prostitute supporters) to engage in self-organization saw their struggle in terms of acting as pressure groups pursuing civil, human and political rights over decriminalization, destigmatization, public awareness, social provisions and social protection (e.g. education, health, welfare) and protection from violence, intimidation and harassment, whether from police, customers or other members of the public. The bodies on which the sex workers and their organizations have sought to exert influence were public opinion, political parties, government, the state and its appendages (e.g. police, judiciary, health, social work).

Several manifestations flow from pursuing this platform in this way. First has been the construction of collectives of sex workers deploying the help, advice and support of various (non-sex worker) professionals and specialists (e.g. lawyers, health care specialists, educationalists). For example, many of these professionals carry out voluntary work for the prostitutes' pressure groups and/or work on funded sex work projects. Second, collective action seeks to win largely individual-based rights and entitlements in the legal and public policy arenas. Third, even where employment issues are directly addressed, sex workers seek to apply pressure on a third party to compel employers to act in a more benign manner. Fourth, the sex worker pressure groups seek to lobby to gain access to the power, resources and influence of the state and various social capital networks rather than attempt to create their own. Thus, the dominant characteristics are acting as ginger groups and being reliant upon others (whether NGOs or the state) to provide either the end goals or the facilitation of these.

Building on this in a different but complimentary manner has been the emergence amongst some sex workers of the view that, as workers, they should organize collectively on the worksite or in the work setting. This is believed to be the more effective way to increase both their individual and collective-based degrees of worksite control and to pursue far more collectively-orientated rights. Indeed, having rights as individual workers is premised on the basis of having collective rights and strength. Consequently, the focus of attention became the immediate employment relationship, the employer and the wage-effort bargain, and no longer just (for example) the police, the legal system or the government. Therefore, attention was given to the terms and conditions of economic exchange in a way that did not exist previously. Moreover, and flowing from this union orientation, there is a thrust to create, and rely on, their own resources to a far greater degree. Although still deploying the expertise of others to some degree, the ability to pay for and secure these results comes from far greater self-organization, self-activity and self-reliance. With self-reliance also comes self-control and independence for the (union) organizations the sex workers establish for themselves.

Labor Unionism

Given that this book is centrally concerned with the unionization of sex workers, it is important to outline a definition of what a labor union is. This is because the normal conception of a labor union in terms of its workplace presence is not necessarily seen as being appropriate for sex workers in quite the same way. This arises from a conception of the union being a workplace union with workplace representatives in fixed and semi-permanent places of work, and where work is also of a fixed and of a semi-permanent nature. Rather, what appears to be more appropriate for sex workers is a form of occupational unionism that regulates the industry at different levels and not just or solely in the workplace.

Nonetheless, the notion of a labor union is important to establish. A union is a voluntary association of citizens like the aforementioned prostitutes' advocacy and rights groups. Its purposes can be many and varied throughout civil society. But the essential rationale of a *labor* union as a union of workers is to reduce competition amongst workers and, thereby, leverage up the terms and conditions given by employers in the wage-effort bargain. This is the sense of strength in numbers. Consequently, a labor union is quintessentially a collective organization *of* workers based in work which focuses upon economic and labor justice through negotiating improved terms for the wage-effort bargain and the organization of work. It does this by creating collective leverage over the employer. As such, a labor union is a relatively tight form of organization compared a more general union of citizens; a labor union is based on the principle of solidarity and its key resource is the collective power of its members, when mobilized through industrial action, at the points (i.e. worksites) of production, distribution and exchange in the economy. However, because workers are the weaker party in the employment relationship with capital, all labor unions also seek to influence the state to regulate employers and capital and, thus, need to intervene in the political arena as well.

Source Materials

The materials for this book come from four sources. First, interviews with sex worker activists and sex worker union activists in Australia, Britain and the United States, and correspondence with sex worker union activists in the other countries studied in this book. Second, writings and reports by sex workers themselves, their organizations and on their activities in terms of their magazines, blogs, websites and postings. This has been particularly useful as sex worker activists have argued and debated over the issues amongst themselves as part of the process of their own development of self-agency. Third, media (both mainstream and radical) coverage of salient events and issues. These media have been keen to cover the issues because they seem 'sexy' and challenging. Finally, there have been studies of some issues of work and employment in sex work by other academics (although none have examined unionization).[3] Where sources are referred to more than once in the endnotes, they are referred to fully the first time and then in an abridged form afterwards. Throughout the book, the term 'industry' is used to collectively describe the selling of sex and sexual services and the labor necessary to do so. Because of the connotations with manufacturing, 'industry' does not seem the most appropriate of terms but it is a widely used one and one which is less cumbersome than describing all the different sectors that comprise the 'industry'. Thus, it is used in this book too.

2

Sex Workers Before Sex Work

The modern prostitutes' – and, thus, sex workers' – movement is commonly believed to have begun with two events in two separate cities, namely, San Francisco in 1973 and Lyon in 1975. In San Francisco, COYOTE (Call Off Your Tired Old Ethics) was founded as the first ever advocacy and pressure group for prostitutes, subsequently operating with the subtitle, 'The Sex Workers' Rights Organization'. In Lyon in 1975, an occupation of a church by prostitutes was carried out to protest against the lack of police vigor in arresting the murderers of prostitutes and lack of adequate police protection for those who continued to work as prostitutes, as well as to oppose the increase in harassment through fines and imprisonment. These two events led to the emergence of a large number of other similar pressure group and advocacy organizations for prostitutes around the world over the next ten to twenty years. Part and parcel of the development of these groups and organization was the emergence of the sex work discourse. In time, these groups campaigning for civil and human rights led to the emergence of proto-unions which concentrated upon the worker, labor and economic rights of sex workers. Therefore, they existed as antecedents that facilitated sex workers defining themselves more widely than just comprising of prostitutes, and provided inspiration for the creation of the organs of collective self-representation of sex workers as workers.[4]

However, there are a number of historically significant antecedents which existed far before the 1970s and that are worth outlining in order to demonstrate that sex work being thought of as work is not solely a product of the post-1970s period. Equally, the antecedents show that, notwithstanding practical difficulties, if sex work is work then sex workers as workers can and should be organized collectively into labor unions. So there is not inconsiderable evidence of sex workers existing in both objective and subjective senses well before and up to the aforementioned breakthroughs in 1973 and 1975.

United States

In the 1880s in Chicago, the Illinois Woman's Alliance, led by labor and socialist activists, campaigned against the police victimization of prostitutes based on a labor relations understanding of prostitution.[5] Possibly helped by this influence, the Industrial Workers of the World (IWW or Wobblies), founded in 1905 in Chicago, had no problem in campaigning for prostitutes' rights or supporting them in collective action. Indeed, its analysis of all problems of oppression linked to class exploitation meant that prostitutes were not stigmatized as might have been expected at this time by radicalized workers and socialists. Moreover, the philosophy of the IWW was that all workers should be enjoined in 'one big union' to, in its words 'smash the boss class'. Prostitutes were, thus, as much entitled to join the 'one big union' as any other workers. Thus, the IWW organized prostitutes in the west of the USA in the early part of the twentieth century as part of their 'one big union' strategy of organizing all workers. The practical emphasis on organizing prostitutes largely concerned organizing workers who were important but ancillary workers to industrial workers. For example, prostitutes were organized to prevent strikebreakers from being allowed to be customers. This was at odds with the view of founding and influential IWW member, Lucy Parsons, who argued for organizing prostitutes as prostitutes in their own right. Indeed, although recognized as workers, the IWW tended to believe women working as prostitutes indicated the inadequacy of male workers' wages such that if male workers' wages were higher, then women working as prostitutes would be unnecessary and consequently families would be able to have women remain in the home to rear children and the like. Evidence of IWW-influenced prostitutes being organized to defend and advance their own interests is less clear. For example, there is some dispute about whether a walkout of prostitutes in New Orleans in April 1907 was organized by the IWW (either non-prostitute or prostitute members) or whether the prostitutes were merely associated with the IWW. Nonetheless, the strike against increase in rents was won when the prostitutes organized pickets of the brothels to stop customers entering and won their demands.[6]

Again in the US, although much later in the century, some burlesque artistes and dancers in the 1940s, 1950s and 1960s were members of the union, the American Guild of Variety Artists (AGVA), which provided them with individual representation.[7] Some reports suggested the famous burlesque artiste Gypsy Rose Lee attempted to unionize burlesque dancers in the early 1950s. Earlier, the Burlesque Artists' Association was reported to be established in 1933. The relationship between the dancers and the AGVA ended in 1973 when the dancers when classified by a court as 'independent contractors'.[8] Around the same time, the Hotel Employees and Restaurant Employees (HERE) union organized Playboy 'bunny girls' in Detroit, gaining a collective bargaining contract there in 1964, and then a national collective bargaining contract for eight Playboy Clubs, covering 500 women 'bunnies', in 1969.[9] These contracts involved the introduction of a wage, for previously the women had earned only tips from customers, and the union was able to contest Hugh Hefner's sole right to determine what attractiveness was in terms of body shape, age, costumes, and so on, as well as gain the introduction of a 'touching rule'. The HERE organizer who initiated the recruitment and recognition drive was Myra Wolfgang.[10] As a labor feminist, she sent her daughter to gain employment at the

Detroit club in order to be a 'salt', namely, an internal spy and organizer for HERE. The campaign took seven months to realize its goal of a union contract in Detroit but longer for a national contract as Hefner organized against HERE.

Canada

Prior to the Canadian Association of Burlesque Entertainers (CABE), there were some sporadic attempts at collectivization and unionization by dancers in Canada. Without normal entitlements like holiday pay, sick leave or pensions, dancers became aggrieved over basic issues of pay and working conditions. For example, in Vancouver in 1967, three 'topless dancers' picketed a club for two nights demanding higher wages, staff privileges, and a dressing room heater. They highlighted the need to organize dancers at other clubs in the city but nothing came of this. An examination of the situation between 1965 and 1980 highlighted that, while various working conditions constituted grievances, the lack of occupational identity, intra-dancer competition and absence of permanent workplaces were three key factors in militating against unionization of dancers.[11] But there were also the forces of employer/operator/agency hostility and opposition from the union movement in regard of seeing sex work as work. The only indications of any similar developments in Britain were two strippers attempting to form a union but being blacklisted from the clubs as a result, and actress and Marxist political activist Vanessa Redgrave touring such clubs in the early to mid-1970s and attempting, without success, to get the strippers to organize themselves into a union or to join her union, Equity, the union for actors.[12]

Conclusion

The importance of these historical antecedents to contemporary sex worker unionization is not founded on any direct linkages. Rather, it is founded upon the saliency of the political perspectives that informed these examples of unionization from the past for contemporary activists today. Intellectually and psychologically, they may be seen to provide inspiration, encouragement and sustenance. For example, that the Playboy 'bunny girls' contested management's right to determine what they looked like and what they wore was of future portent, as this book will highlight, with regard to dancers and prostitutes. And unionized 'bunnies', led by Myra Wolfgang, fused workers' rights together with women's rights. But the use of 'independent contract' or self-employed status in burlesque also headed up what would be a powerful practical and ideological challenge to labor unionism for sex workers in the decades ahead.

3

Sex Worker Union Organizing Stateside

The US is an obvious place to start a survey of contemporary sex worker unionization. It has one of the biggest domestic sex industries in the world as a result of the size of its population, economy and particular culture. However, in another sense it is not an obvious starting place, for unions are very weak in the US, with private sector density having been below 10% since the late 1990s. Indeed, it was never very high even in the heyday of union influence in the 1970s, being 25% in 1975. Most of the attempts at collective organization involve exotic dancers and not prostitutes or other sex workers. The most obvious amongst many reasons for this is that prostitution is unlawful in the vast majority of US states. The attempts that have been made have been conceived in *union* terms with the focus far less on public morality and public policy and far more on work and employment terms and conditions.

Exotic Dancers: First Beginnings

From 1980 onwards, there has been a frequent and ever-recurring number of cases of exotic dancers attempting to unionize themselves to fight for better working conditions and control over their working lives. Of the first three known cases, one was met with physical violence – presumed murder – and another management intimidation, while the third petered out through apparent lack of interest.[13] At this time dancers being employees – rather than 'independent contractors' - was the norm, but this would shortly change with significant ramifications.

Topless dancers, along with bouncers, bartenders and DJs at a San Diego club engaged in union organizing in 1993 as a result of grievances over pay and conditions. Although paid an hourly rate and shift bonus, dancers were forced to pay per hour to work, compulsorily tip other staff and buy dancing costumes from the club with the effect that, some nights, dancers ended up owing the club more money than they earned. The dancers contacted the HERE union. Initially, it was sceptical because of its inexperience of this sector, high dancer turnover rates and their irregular shifts. But it was persuaded the dancers were workers and performing work. With its help, enough signatures were quickly gained to file a National Labor Relations Board (NLRB) application for union recognition. The first ballot was lost but the second was not. But the club resisted, firing one of the lead dancer organizers and worsening working conditions as a punishment for the second vote. It hoped to take advantage of the turnover in dancers and create demoralization. Over a year later, however, the club relented and agreed to a first bargaining contract. While it provided for basic protection from unfair treatment and victimization, the club would not shift on the hourly 'fee' charge and raised this by 1100% and fired the second lead dancer organizer. Two years later, the dancers voted to derecognize the union after becoming unhappy over its ability to represent their interests.

Established in 1993 in San Francisco, the Exotic Dancers' Alliance (EDA) sought to tackle the issues of working conditions, especially the introduction of stage fees and self-employed status. The issues crystallized around a keenly felt lack of collective 'voice' for dancers. Innovatively, it used many workplace posters to address dancers with slogans like 'Stop looking for support in the lingerie department', 'Like an orgy, it only works if there's a lot of us' and 'United we stand – divided we bend over'. The notion to collectivize came from a realization that a permanent – rather than one-off – form of collective organization was necessary. But like all subsequent attempts at unionization in the US, the dancers ran into two problems. One was that they were increasingly classified as 'independent contactors' and, thus, not eligible to avail themselves of the (limited) rights of workers in the US. In particular, one of these rights concerned the ability to use the NLRB to organize a ballot for union recognition. If the ballot is won, then the employer is legally compelled to collectively bargain over terms and conditions of employment. However, this right is only afforded to employees. The second was that the practice of labor unionism in the US is not 'open source' unionism. In other words, unions in the US tend only organize workers where they are working under union-negotiated contracts or are trying to unionize the whole of a workforce to gain a contract. Consequently, organizing relatively small numbers where collective bargaining is not undertaken is not the habit of US unions.

One of the ways the EDA tried to get round these problems was to become a union itself and show that, in doing so, it was trying to organize employees. The battle to establish dancers as *de facto* employees became central to its attempt – and all subsequent attempts – at unionization. It centered upon whether the work they undertook was the same as, similar, or comparable to the work of employees, in terms of how management not only managed and supervised their labor but also dictated what was performed, as well as directing how it was performed and the terms upon which it would be carried out. If this could be demonstrated, then the dancers could show they lacked the control, independence and autonomy that non-employees like independent contractors have. In the course of the battle the EDA began, its two main activists were essentially sacked by being continually told when they turned up for their shifts that the shifts were full and the club did not need any more dancers that day.

The EDA submitted complaints about working conditions to the Market Street Cinema Club and state bodies which examined and regulated employment matters, as well as making contact with the Service Employees International Union (SEIU). In 1994, the EDA secured its first success with a ruling from the Labor Commission that dancers were not 'independent contractors', with the Market Street Cinema being ordered to pay back wages and return stage fees. However, the club increased its stage fees and appealed against the ruling. Meantime, a group of dancers at another club organized themselves together and called upon management to reduce the stage fees. This was refused so the dancers filed a complaint with the NLRB. Again this led to the realization of the need to operate as a union through the EDA. The club then 'sacked' the dancers that joined the SEIU in 1995, while at a third club in 1997 an attempt to unionize was met by closure after the dancers joined the SEIU. However, the EDA was successful in organizing several class action lawsuits to get the return of stage fees at a number of other clubs. But various clubs prohibited distribution of EDA material (like the aforementioned posters), and sacked and blacklisted EDA activists and members. The EDA then succeed in 2000 in gaining a change in Californian law so that dancers were classified as employees and not compelled to pay stage fees. But again clubs devised new and legal means by which to charge dancers *de facto* upfront fees.

Other dancers opposed the EDA, with some setting up the Independent Dancers' Association, Strippers to Retire into Prosperity (STRIP) and the Strippers' Society of San Francisco, being fearful that employed status would reduce the number of opportunities for dancers and their earnings as clubs hired less and charged higher fees. This opposition, along with burnout of the key activists, led the EDA to shut its doors by late 2004. But before this, the EDA played a crucial part in unionizing the Lusty Lady. The vacuum left by the EDA was attempted to be filled by a small group called Sex Workers Organized for Labor, Human and Civil Rights (SWOLHCR).

Lusty Lady

The Lusty Lady, a San Francisco peepshow, is the only unionized sex club in the US. Despite paternalistic management and employed status, since the mid-1980s there had been talk about unionization, even a strike, and isolated attempts to organize. Tendencies to discuss unionization grew as the club began to control dancers' appearance and behavior more tightly – since, because it employed the dancers, it could not use the market for customers' tips alone to determine these facets – and this led to an increasing number of dismissals. With renewed vigor as a result of the arrival of several new dancers in the early 1990s, the conditions for a concerted unionizing attempt were laid.

Dancers began organizing in 1993 primarily as a result of grievances about customers filming or photographing them without their knowledge, consent or compensation, and favoritism in dancer selection for shifts.[14] They were immensely aided in doing so by having employed status, by not being in direct competition with each other, given hourly wages, and by the presence of sex worker feminists. At the outset, organizing was not conceived in union terms until one of the dancers attended an EDA meeting held at an SEIU office in 1996. This led to meetings to discuss prospects of organizing the Lusty based on an agreement between the EDA and SEIU whereby the SEIU would support the EDA representing any strippers in San Francisco who wanted to unionize. The Lusty dancers were pleased to learn this even though they had not decided to unionize at this point. However, upon realizing that they had very few rights unless unionized, they began a unionization drive.

Upon hearing of the drive, the club responded by removing the remaining offending one-way mirrored booths and, hiring a law firm, went on the offensive. This merely galvanized the dancers further into making an NLRB application for a union recognition ballot. Management prepared for the ballot by running an anti-union propaganda campaign. The underlying messages were: the union cannot be trusted, it has separate interests from workers or its members, and it's an unaccountable third-party. Two key activists were placed on 'final warnings' for bogus infractions. The club also began to take on more dancers in an attempt to reduce the proportion of unionized dancers. Despite all this and pleas to give the club a second chance, the ballot was won and in 1997 the EDA at the Lusty became the Exotic Dancers' Union (EDU) chapter of the SEIU. The chapter was led by the dancers but also included cashiers, janitors and security staff.

However, this victory was merely the first battle in a long war. 'Surface' or 'bad faith' bargaining was practiced by the club, so to break this logjam the dancers took a form of industrial action called 'No Pink', where no genitals were shown during dancing. In response, management fired a dancer, to which the others responded by picketing the club and chanting 'Two, four, six, eight, don't come here to masturbate!' Management retaliated with a lockout, closing the club. After a two-day stalemate, and surprised by the dancers' collective strength, management backed down, rehired the dancer and began bargaining. The contract comprised a formal grievance procedure, binding arbitration, an improved wage scale, a sick pay scheme, one day's holiday a year, employment security and no discrimination due to race, hair color or breast size. Equally significant was that the EDU/SEIU negotiated a second contract in 1998 which improved on the first.

The Lusty 'story' took another significant turn when the dancers and support workers bought the club, transforming it in to an employee-owned enterprise or workers' cooperative. Shortly after signing of a new two-year collective bargaining contract in 2003, the owners announced they intended to close it down because of increasing wages costs and the hassle of labor disputes. Upon hearing this, the dancers (and other staff) decided to buy the business. Their motivation was not just to save jobs but to take the opportunity to work for themselves, own the 'means of the production' as they put it, own a business and run it as they wished. Union recognition and union membership were retained because not all staff were employee-owners and because of uncertainty over the future of the business.

But shortly after becoming a cooperative, the Lusty came under pressure to make financial cost savings. Revenue dropped while the loan to buy the business required repaying. And the consequences for membership participation as a result of staff turnover leading to a loss of technical and social capital, along with the extra effort and transaction costs for workers involved in running a cooperative, quickly became apparent. These difficulties were compounded and extended by a bitter internal feud. In 2006, a number of male support workers tried to derecognize the EDU/SEIU against a backdrop of internal strife, ranging from inflammatory emails and verbal communications, suspensions, firings and competing allegations from dancers and support staff of sexual harassment and unfair labor practices. This began when some of the male workers, who are front desk and cleaning staff (and coop members), began arguing that the coop was losing money (which impacted on wage levels and job security) because the dancers were too fat, big and un-sexy, and that the union contract was invalid because the coop made no distinction between management and labor. This outraged the dancers, who regarded the views of these male workers as discriminatory and rolling back the gains of the hard-fought battle to unionize the Lusty. In the process, a considerable divide opened up between the cooperative board of management, generally supporting the business case argument of the male workers, and the SEIU which supported the dancers. However, subsequently these tensions eased, aided by the cooperative's financial position improving as a result of dancer initiatives and staff turnover amongst non-dancers. To this day, the Lusty remains in business, still as the only unionized and worker cooperative sex club.

The Lusty's Impact

The Lusty's counterpart in Seattle experienced an unsuccessful organizing drive shortly after that of its sister club. The grievances and context were similar. What appear to have been the critical 'missing' components were those of a determined number of sex worker union activists and less collective confidence amongst dancers in unionization (because of the belief the union caused conflict between dancers and club). However, the club also tried to preempt unionization by raising wages, creating a staff forum and having staff reps. Yet following the success at the Lusty in San Francisco, the EDA reported shows of interest from dancers in Oregon, Washington, New York, Pittsburgh, Philadelphia, Florida, Texas, Kansas, Massachusetts and southern California. However, few progressed into union organizing drives of any significance. In addition to reasons of employer/operator intimidation, some of the explanation for this is that improvements in conditions were won by collective efforts without a union and by individual dancers taking out lawsuits against their employers/operators (see below).

Two shows of interest that did lead to union organizing drives were in Anchorage, Alaska, and Philadelphia. Dancers and staff at the Showboat in Anchorage started organizing a union, the Alaskan Exotic Dancers' Union, in 1997 in response to rising club fees and unsafe working conditions. The dancers approached the Teamsters' union and gained help from it but were abandoned mid-way through the campaign for union recognition,[15] whereupon the dancers found help from HERE instead. Management responded by firing the activists, increasing house fees, imposing a one-day lock-out, and subjecting pro-union workers to threats and harassment. With the Hell's Angels believed to control the club, this presence added to the level of intimidation.[16] But rather than weather the lengthy appeals process involved in litigating against unfair labor practice charges through the NLRB, the Alaska Exotic Dancers Union through HERE opted instead to negotiate a settlement (involving back wages, reinstatement of sacked activists and a pledge to desist from interfering or intimidating any future unionization drives). But the settlement did not require the club to recognize the union or collectively bargain. Although the activists viewed the settlement as merely the first step in the continuing campaign and petitioned the NLRB to hold a ballot, it became clear that the club had managed to frighten off the majority of dancers from supporting the union as no petition or election were forthcoming.

A dancer in Philadelphia organized her co-workers to fight for union recognition in 1997. She had been organizing around grievances of wage levels, dressing room facilities, irregular hours and inconsistent application of discipline. The Teamsters' union helped collect signatures, file an application with the NLRB and begin campaigning for the vote but then abandoned the effort without notice.[17] In the ballot, the union dancers failed to gain a majority as a result of management intimidation. The lead dancer organizers were physically threatened by the manager and two were fired but then reinstated. The NLRB substantiated the claims of the death threats, intimidation and harassment prior to the ballot. Others were denied shifts for supporting unionization. The NLRB sought a court order forcing the employer to bargain with the dancers' Professional Dancers Union. But further threats of sacking, blacklisting and club closure led the organizing attempt to wither rapidly thereafter. After suing, the lead sacked dancer organizer gained back pay. Later in Philadelphia in 2002, ten dancers came together to form the Sex Workers' Action Team (SWAT) to try to improve dancers' working conditions and overall standing in the community. They wanted to form a union but were wary of being victimized as other dancers had recently been fired by two clubs.[18] Although SWAT held some fundraisers, it and its desire for unionization did not progress and withered and died.

Back in San Francisco, frustration with the inward-looking orientation of Lusty union members – concerning themselves only with Lusty issues – and lack of SEIU help in unionizing other sex workers, led a number of activists to establish SWOLCHR. It continued the campaign against stage fees and compulsion to prostitute in lapdancing clubs, helped file class law actions to recoup stage fees, and made representations to the California Labor Commission. But it disintegrated as a result of the victimization of its main activist, Daisy Anarchy. She catalogued the retribution that was meted out to her and others in a submission to City Hall in San Francisco in 2005. This included in 1997 being fired by a club along with another activist for 'political activity', the other activist being fired by another club in 1999 when contacted by this previous club (which was the subject of an unfair labor practice complaint to the NLRB), Daisy being fired in 2001 by another club for exposing a manager there for pimping and pandering, a club manager attending a union meeting for dancers in 2002 in order to intimidate them, and a chain of clubs in 2004 using the 'captive audience' meeting tactic for union busting.

Subsequent to this, the Erotic Service Providers' Union (EPSU) in 2004 tried to take up the cudgels in San Francisco. It collected signatures to allow its proposal to get on a public ballot to facilitate a bill on decriminalizing prostitution in San Francisco – narrowly losing the proposal when put to the public vote – gave testimony to the city's Entertainment Commission on a proposed amendment to the Police Code for the regulation of live adult entertainment businesses, and submitted evidence to the Commission on the Status of Women. Despite the ESPU working in conjunction with the local Labor Council to prose-lytize amongst sex workers for labor unionism and train sex worker activists in labor union skills, it is essentially a union in name and aspiration rather than reality.

Since the ESPU's establishment, a dancer in Georgia was harassed by the FBI on account of a number of issues including her IWW membership. She commented; 'The IWW ... [is] the only union that takes strippers. That's why I joined. For a while I was thinking about organizing the strippers in Atlanta, but I ran into some hostility when I was trying to do it'.[19] Then in 2010, a dancer in Washington had a grievance over being required to pay stage fees and fines as well as tip other staff. In the course of trying to take a lawsuit against the club, she began contemplating forming a union for dancers. Upon hearing this, the club told her to 'get in line' and effectively fired her.[20] However being fired and meeting opposition from other dancers for 'rocking the boat' stymied this initiative to create a union.

Las Vegas Dancers' Alliance

The Las Vegas Dancers' Alliance (LVDA) was founded in 2002 by an exotic dancer who was a former union activist at Boeing aircraft manufacturers. Initially, the LDVA had just over 100 members but some nine months later this was reported to be around 1,000 members out of around 15,000 dancers working in Las Vegas and 35,000 in the adjacent Clark County, with clandestine workplace reps operating in two thirds of the lapdancing clubs in Las Vegas.[21] Following its founding, the LVDA provided help to nude dancers in Texas and spoke of its aspiration to found a United States Dancers' Alliance. The stimulus to the LVDA was the passing of new lapdancing regulations which, as a result of their no-touching rule and the exorbitant cost of holding a dancing license, had deleterious implications for dancers' earnings. Thus, the LDVA was not conceived as a union but as a pressure group to repeal the new regulations and to act as a defender of the adult entertainment industry per se and the business of dancers.[22] But being spurned by the clubs in trying to do so, and a realization of the need to focus upon working conditions, turned it into a union. Consequently, the LDVA sought to negotiate a health insurance scheme for members but this proved unsuccessful since the dancers were deemed to be independent contractors. Thus, the LDVA campaigned to have dancers reclassified as club employees, using the evidence of club's control of dancers' working time and work organization.

Club owners became enraged at the prospect of being forced to employ dancers given the reduction in revenue and increase in costs incurred. They were further enraged by the loss of power they would have as this would effectively end their ability to contract dancers to work in sufficient numbers to create competition amongst them for work and custom. Consequently, LVDA activists were subject to intimidation. One filed an unfair labor practice charge to the NLRB after being drugged, robbed, threatened and arrested while the LVDA leader was sacked from two different clubs, blacklisted from some and barred from entering others. With a number of setbacks, the LVDA became less active and then disintegrated as its leader left the industry to find work elsewhere. Indeed, a sympathetic article in the *Las Vegas Review Journal* in 2005[23] on dancers' need for a union did not even mention either the LVDA or any successor, even though the leader of the LVDA had written to the paper less than six months before.[24] Along the way, no established union in Las Vegas offered any tangible help.[25] The Sin City Alternative Professionals' Association (SCAPA), founded in 2004, is not a successor organization to the LVDA as it is the Las Vegas chapter of the Sex Workers Outreach Project USA and is, thus, an advice and support group in the mould of COYOTE. Although it believes in sex workers' labor rights, SCAPA's roles concern the provision of business and employment information, education and skills training on sex work for sex workers.

Organizing in Porn Valley

The vast majority of US film and video porn is produced in California's San Fernando Valley as a result of a decision by the California Supreme Court in 1988 over pornography falling within the ambit of the constitutional right of free speech. Frequent attempts have been made to organize the actors and actresses since then. But even before San Fernando became the locus for this production, there were initiatives to unionize the actors and actresses. The first known ones date back to the 1970s, revolving around the decision by the established union, the Screen Actors' Guild (SAG), in 1974, not to organize porn. This decision related to the furore around *Deep Throat*, whether porn was acting and professional acting, and, critically, the SAG's policy only to recruit members working on films where a collective bargaining contract (over terms and conditions) exists between itself and the production company. Consequently, all subsequent attempts to unionize have either concerned trying to change SAG policy from the outside or trying to set up new and entirely self-resourced independent unions. This has meant that a double hurdle has had to be straddled by those trying to unionize the 1,000-1,500 actors and actress in San Fernando Valley.

Nina Hartley and a number of other porn actresses in the late 1980s established The Pink Ladies' Social Club to generate discussion about performers' rights and interests, including the issue of establishing a professional or union organization. The group met and published a newsletter. Hostility from the SAG and threats from production companies about those involved not working again or experiencing acts of violence helped explain why nothing came of the discussions. However, the idea would not go away and was frequently stimulated by the outbreak of HIV infections, which highlighted how vulnerable performers were to the consequences of poor working conditions. Specifically, the low usage of condoms increased the likelihood of infections breaking out and put vital importance upon a robust and enforced regime of regular HIV (and other STD) testing.

In 1997, porn actress Dalny Marga Valdes tried to join the SAG in order to get industrial bargaining coverage to gain income on royalties on her work, but was refused membership as the SAG stated the sector she worked in was not part of mainstream entertainment. She then filed a complaint to the NLRB against the SAG but was unsuccessful. This highlighted again that porn is essentially produced by independent companies which are non-union and that the SAG does not operate by 'open source' unionism. In the same year, there were calls for the formation of a union when actress Nena Cherry contracted HIV. This was also the stimulus for the founding in 1998 of the Erotic Entertainers' Guild. Organized by a small number of activists including the then-reigning female 'Performer of the Year', Johnnie Black, and her husband, David Johnson, the Guild met just a few times, issued a newsletter and began campaigning on sexual health issues. However, those involved balked at the scale of the task facing them – not only establishing a new union from scratch but also unionizing their fellow workers, particularly when the attempt to establish minimum wage rates through the Guild was met by performers showing that they were willing to undercut each other to get work.[26] A year later, the Guild had disintegrated.

Then, in 2003, a group of performers led by actor Mr. Marcus – who was involved in the Erotic Entertainers' Guild – established the Adult Performers' Union. However, nothing further emerged despite reported meetings with the Teamsters' union. Following an HIV outbreak in 2004, some forty performers, including Tony Tedeschi, met several times to draw up a list of demands concerning healthcare, pay and working hours. Testing provision and certification *vis-à-vis* employers' responsibility were viewed as inadequate and work was paid by scene or day rates with little limit on the number of hours and no overtime.

The group, which proposed to establish a union called Adult Entertainment Workers, contacted the American Federation of Television and Radio Artists to see if they could offer assistance but the request was not taken seriously. Out of this proto-union, ATRIBE (Adult Talents Rights in Being Exclusive) was also established as another means of trying to secure a fair return for performers' labor. In late 2007, actress Katie Gold made another attempt to organize a porn actors' union but to no avail.

Along the way, porn star Jenna Jameson called for a union to be established after an actor tested HIV positive in 2010.[27] She argued: 'There's going to have to be a union put in place, and having safe sex is mandatory'. This highlighted that although Californian law requires condoms or equivalent protection on sets and the California Occupational Safety and Health Agency (Cal-OSHA) successfully fined companies for breaking the law, unless an actor complains to Cal-OSHA, Cal-OSHA finds it difficult to intervene. But performers fear being blacklisted if they insist upon protection or make complaints in another instance of the 'race to the bottom'. The point Jameson was making was that with union protection, performers would feel more confident to insist on condom usage or make complaints without retribution. The continual HIV outbreaks indicate that the self-regulation of the industry – through the production companies – of performers being required to test every 30 days for HIV and STDs at an industry-allied clinic has not been working. For example, a performer can test negative in the morning, get infected later that day through work or personal life and work for a month with HIV.

The return of heightened sensitivity about HIV led to the Adult Performers Association (APA) being established by producer/director Nica Noelle and performer January Seraph in 2011. Specifically, it was stimulated by collapse of AIM earlier in the year and the paucity of health insurance. In its own words: 'APA is an organization of adult performers and our supporters who are passionate about improving health, safety and quality of life for adult film entertainers. We endeavor to reach these and other goals through education, encouragement, advocacy, resources and support. ... The APA is designed to improve the lives of Adult Industry Performers, but we believe everyone in the industry will benefit from our research and efforts. We intend to address health and safety conditions in the workplace, to educate performers on their rights, facilitate dialogue with agents, producers and studios, and rework our outdated and inaccurate image in the mainstream press. Our ultimate goal is that Adult Performers will have access to healthcare, and develop a sense of security and empowerment through education, improved work conditions, and reduced social stigma'.[28] This suggests APA saw itself more in terms of a friendly or benevolent society and professional association combined, rather than as a labor union.

Bill Margold, longstanding porn actor and one-time proselytizer for unionization in porn, likened trying to unionize performers to herding cats.[29] There are certainly the forces of competition to gain work, wealth and celebrity and the increasing numbers seeking work in the sector to contend with. But these are far from the only factors – others are the transient nature of the workforce with few performers having much longevity in the sector, performers working in other parts of the sex industry to supplement their incomes so that their focus is not solely porn, performers being compelled to sign contracts which excuse producers from any liabilities, and some of them having rather chaotic personal lives so that organizing is not their forte. However, there are further obstacles to be contended with, such as there being no fixed workplaces, the nature of short-term project work, the power of the producers under self-regulation of the sector, the rise of free porn putting pressure on revenues, and so on. Yet none of these obstacles are necessarily insuperable, as the Writers' Guild of American and SAG indicate, for they exist in many similar circumstances of writers and actors not being employed at all (much less on permanent contracts) and in fixed locations. The main way in which they have dealt with the challenges they face is to become occupational unions which represent a distinct profession and to exercise extra-workplace influence by establishing a form of industry regulation.

Prostitutes

There have been very few instances of attempts by prostitutes to unionize themselves. Carol Leigh recounted being involved in organizing one in the 1980s that did not develop.[30] In the meantime, a prostitute reported being involved in organizing a prostitutes' strike at the American Massage Parlor over macho-management and long working hours as well as applying to the NLRB for union recognition at the next brothel in which she gained employment.[31] The employer sacked the striking prostitutes. Finally, BDSM sex workers in New York in 2008 established a political action committee called DomPAC with a view to paving the way to unionization in order to gain health insurance and unemployment benefits.[32] The sparseness of attempts to organize prostitutes, among other factors, is related to the legal status of prostitution so that what Margo St. James, founder of COYOTE, argued in the 1970s – that 'a union for prostitutes is not possible now. One could not even dream of starting a union without opening oneself up to a lot of legal problems'[33] – still remains true.[34] Thus, unionizing prostitutes could lead to charges being laid against prostitutes under conspiracy laws. Consequently, the establishment by the IWW in 1995 of the Sex Trade Workers Industrial Union 690 for all those employed as dancers and models, telephone sex workers, actors and other workers who use sexuality as the primary tool of their trade made no difference either.[35]

Non-Union Routes

In recounting and analyzing attempts to create collectivism through unions, it is important not to lose sight of other forms of collective-interest representation, some of which are independent and not necessarily at odds with labor unionism. The main form of action here is a class action lawsuit (which is not necessarily the preserve of non-union collectivism). It has been used by exotic dancers in a large number of states to try to stop the charging of stage fees, gain repayment of these, establish an hourly wage, and gain recognition in law of employed status (thus becoming entitled to rights for unfair dismissal, unemployment benefit, and so on). Such cases have taken place in Anchorage, San Diego, San Francisco, Dallas, Denver, Los Angeles, Minneapolis, Las Vegas, Pittsburgh, Portland and Washington. In Oregon in 1995, the case established that dancers were employees but this was appealed, while the ones in Anchorage in 1987, Dallas in 1992 and Minneapolis in 1994 recognized dancers as employees. In Minneapolis, the class lawsuit by 150 dancers recovered back wages under the state's Fair Labor Standards Act and established they were entitled to the minimum wage, leading the club to offer an out-of-court settlement through third-party arbitration. The basis of these lawsuits was that dancers are employees because their supposed freedom as independent contractors is so heavily constrained in terms of when they work, their length of shifts, music they dance to, obligatory tipping of other staff, and so on. However, the direction of traffic has not always been one way. In another case in Portland, Oregon, an exotic dancer took a lawsuit against a club in 2009 for not paying minimum hourly wage and forcing payment of stage fees to dance (or take cut of tips). In 2010, the case was lost when court ruled that the dancer was an independent contractor, not an employee, when she worked at Exotica International Club for Men as Exotica did not control her schedule or the hours she worked, nor did the club dictate what she wore, how she danced or the amount she charged for private dances. Despite this, some clubs stopped charging stage fees and provided better working conditions[36] although others have 'fired' dancers for taking similar legal actions against them.

A second type of collective action that is non-law based has been that of loose, fluid and relatively passive community networks. These networks are as much support networks as they are campaigning organizations. One example in the 1990s was 'Club 90' where 'members' met to talk and discuss their work and working conditions. Online sites like *Bound, Not Gagged, exoticdancernet, stripperweb* and *stripperpower* have also existed in this way, as have the now defunct *Danzine* and *$pread* magazines. By contrast, the Desiree Alliance, a coalition of sex workers and health and educational professionals formed in 2005, is a much more active organization in advocating for sex workers' human, labor and civil rights. The centerpiece of its activities is its annual conference. A different type of non-union route has emerged elsewhere based not on collective self-organization but on alliances with operators and owners over bans on touching and no-touching rules. Both fearing loss of income, operators and dancers formed campaigns to try to reverse the local and state ordinances. However, there were also some cases where dancers collectivized independently to do so, as in the case of Ohio dancers in 2007 forming the Dancers for Freedom and Democracy group and organizing a mass petition.

Conclusion

The case of sex workers unionizing in the US demonstrates that there has been a sufficient and continual number of attempts to suggest that a pattern exists, namely, there is a desire – an unmet desire – for union representation. It is clearly grievance-based rather than being merely ideological. However, with a small number of activists at their center, the attempts at unionization have been liable to decapitation techniques from operators and owners. In the US, these are far from uncommon. Indeed, every 23 minutes a worker was fired or victimized between 1993 and 2003 for being a union member. By 2005, this figure was one every 17 minutes.[37] Legal recourse for this is weak and only open to employees. Consequently, it is not just loss of anonymity that sex workers face by becoming union activists but also retribution. In this context, it is a testament to those that have been prepared to put their heads above the parapet. One key way to reduce the possibility of retribution and the chances of effective union representation is to develop a form of occupational labor unionism (see subsequent chapters).

4

Sex Worker Unionization in Britain

This chapter examines the unionization of sex workers in Britain since the late 1990s. It consequently, and almost exclusively, focuses upon the London-based International Union of Sex Workers (IUSW) and the GMB general union adult entertainment branch. The IUSW was established in 2000 in London as a result of a series of events and processes which brought together a number of sex workers with a belief in the need to form a collective organization to represent the interests of sex workers. One spur was that although the longstanding English Collective of Prostitutes is often called the 'girls' union', it is not a union and does not seek to organize and represent sex workers *per se*. Another was the belief in the power of social movements and social movement unionism for workers' representation.

Having established the IUSW, its activists realized not only did they need to be, and act as, a *union* but they should also be part of the wider *union* movement in order to benefit from its resources. Initially, they approached the Transport and General Workers' Union (TGWU) to discuss the possibility of their members joining but this was rebuffed. Approaches to the Trades Union Congress (TUC) were also spurned with the IUSW dismissed as being deviant and legitimizing sexism and women's oppression. Then it approached the GMB general union and the response of its London region was sympathetic and supportive. On the basis of the IUSW encouraging its members to join the GMB, of IUSW members only being eligible to the benefits of the GMB once GMB members and not acting contrary to GMB policies, the IUSW was able to help establish in 2002 the GMB adult entertainment branch. The IUSW remains closely linked to the GMB but is more akin to a sex worker advocacy and rights group and it is in this context that its aspiration of being an international union of sex workers must be seen.

Recruitment and Organizing

Since the GMB adult entertainment branch was launched, it has grown slowly but steadily in membership. It rose from forty in late 2002 to around two hundred by the end of 2003. However, by early 2006 nearly 2,000 sex workers were GMB members.[38] This was then a far larger number of members than the IUSW, particularly because the IUSW is a *de facto* network of activists and not a membership-based organization as such. Prominent blogger, writer, feminist and Unison union activist, Cath Elliot, criticized the IUSW for masquerading as a union when amongst its members were some sex industry operators.[39] This rather missed the point because the IUSW is not a union. However, the criticism did highlight that in a situation when a union – the GMB in this case – is a nascent one for the sector concerned, one of the ways it tries to get a foothold in the sector from a position of weakness is to work with employers and operators on common interests (see below).

Growth in GMB membership resulted from deploying of a series of campaigning tools. One was the use of high levels of media profile to reach potential members, given the lack of resources the GMB and sex worker union activists have and the wide distribution of sex workers throughout Britain (and where many are not obviously visible). Another was to operate through appropriate and conducive fora and milieus such as the Sexual Freedom Coalition, UK Network of Sex Work Projects, sexual health organizations and sex workers' health projects. This is because traditional, direct union recruitment at the entrances to workplaces is not always possible given that many are not visible and sex workers' worksites are not fixed as many other workers' workplaces are. In the cases of Majingos and Club Crème (see below), access facilitated by the employer was important. Such means helped overcome the challenge of finding the sex workers and also the issue of unfamiliarity, by coming through some known and trusted avenues.

Lapdancing: Art of the Possible?

There some three hundred lapdancing clubs in Britain in 2011, having grown from two hundred in 2002 following a relaxation of licensing laws in 2003.[40] Each club may have up to 200 dancers on its 'books'. Of all the advances the GMB has made, union recognition agreements, workplace union organization, and working relationships with managements in a small number of clubs represent the pinnacle of its achievements. *Labour Research* reported: 'The GMB has been recognized in three table/lapdancing clubs in the UK, and these workers now have union and health and safety reps, negotiated contracts and grievance procedures established'.[41] Two of these clubs were Majingos and Club Crème. Other than the supportive attitudes of the management in the two clubs, the GMB has been able to make use of the relatively concentrated location of sex workers in defined and more accessible workplaces where, despite the use of self-employment rather than direct employment, a more tangible link and form of identity exists between dancers and clubs. Moreover, with the recent expansion of lapdancing, the relative respectability given to this activity has increased so that such a 'cloud of shame' does not surround it as is still the case with prostitution. In this sense, reduced stigmatization affords a relatively easier opening for labor unionism.

Majingos, in Canary Wharf, east London, was the first club in Britain to have its dancers unionized and the first to grant union recognition. Opened in 2002, the club management has relatively progressive views with regard to workers' rights and how these support the Majingos brand as a high-end, quality club which does not have problems with the local council getting its license renewed. Thus, its general manager invited the GMB to attend dancer auditions with a view to recruiting those that came to work at the club. Of the advances made at Majingos, the foremost has been 'no-touching' of dancers' code of conduct for customers, where transgression leads to removal, and a code of conduct which on the issue of dancer drinking states: 'The management insists on moderate drinking at all times. However, do not refuse a drink when offered. You do not have to drink it.' If the code is believed to have been broken, there is a right to be represented and a right to appeal in order to present victimization or termination of working.[42] Nonetheless, dancers are not employed, they still pay stage fees and only earn money from doing private dances so that stage dancing is merely a 'shop window'.

Club Crème in Bristol became the second unionized and union-recognized club. Following a meeting in 2002 organized by the club for all dancers in the city at which the GMB was invited to attend to recruit dancers, nearly half joined the GMB hearing about the success at Majingos even though they had no particular grievances with the club. Nonetheless, those that joined emphasized that unionization could help improve conditions and provide a safer working environment across the sex industry (such as dances in private booths without security). The GMB gained union recognition quickly because of a sympathetic management attitude. Again, this stemmed from management support for workers' right and how this reinforced their brand and business case (like recruiting and retaining good dancers).

The attitude of these clubs compares quite starkly with that of the major chains, like Spearmint Rhino, where cooperation and recognition of common interests have been absent. Although earnings may be high – providing a disincentive for joining[43] – and some 'house mothers' play a maternal role towards their dancers, there has also been an anti-union approach from a number of clubs including those that favor sector-wide regulation to maintain standards and respectability.[44] This situation may arise because the larger chains and clubs have the resources to maintain standards and respectability without needing the GMB's help. Moreover, the over-hiring of dancers creates a situation where there is competition to gain earnings from customers, putting dancers in a weak position. Even protecting employment by the GMB campaigning with clubs against closure[45] under new licensing laws has not necessarily advanced workers' rights within these clubs when kept open. Indeed, the intensity of employer/operator fury when their right to manage as they see fit is challenged was highlighted by a dancer claiming unfair dismissal against Stringfellows.[46] This became a test case for the industry because the basis of claiming unfair dismissal was to be able to show that the dancer had *de facto* employment with the club because her shifts were rostered by the club and she was barred from working elsewhere.

Equity, the actors' union, stated it was surprised that the GMB sought to organize pole and table dancers because it believed that such workers fell within its remit.[47] However, it was not until 2007 that Equity sought to organize pole dancers as professional entertainment artists with a number joining (as part of its move to unionize models used in fashion and advertising). Their grievances related to long hours, contracts, body size and establishing minimum standards.

Organizing the industry

The GMB estimated there were some 250,000 sex workers in Britain in 2003.[48] With its small sex worker membership and which is based mainly in London, the task facing the GMB in organizing sex workers is huge and daunting. Recognizing this weakness, the GMB's approach has been to trying the strategy of 'organizing the industry'. By this, it does not mean trying to organize each and every worksite but rather exert influence on the industry through a number of levers to assist defending and advancing members' interests and become the recognized voice of sex workers through having a *sufficient* number of members - several thousand - and, thus, being a player in the industry. Consequently, it has sought to use other levers of potential influence that exists above and beyond the worksite. Thus, one has been to try to establish a regime of voluntary regulation through notions of 'industry labor standards' rather than collective bargaining in the first instance. This involves trying to form a coalition with employers and interested parties such as advocacy groups in a *quid quo pro* over creating a legitimate image for the industry and a wider, unified lobbying force for the industry. By seeking to work with the 'good' employers, the GMB hopes to marginalize the 'bad', and ultimately put them out of business, thus levelling up working conditions. For the 'good' employers, working with the GMB may force the 'bad' employers to adopt better practices, preventing the latter from gaining competitive advantage through lower costs (or alternatively putting them out of business through increased costs). 'Good employers' may also hope to protect themselves from government intervention through either cleaning up the industry's image and/or ensuring that intervention was targeted solely on reprehensible operators. However, it has become clear over time that the GMB has not yet got to the position of membership strength where it can credibly offer those amenable employers such a deal. This is in no small part due to the hostility of many of the clubs to GMB membership. Thus, the GMB finds itself in a veritable'Catch-22' position.

Unionized Brothel

In 2003, a massage parlor in Stoke-on-Trent became the first brothel in Britain to become unionized and have *de facto* union recognition. The brothel owner along with the five prostitutes working there joined the GMB following her and two of the prostitutes having attended the IUSW/GMB foundation meeting in London in 2002. The brothel had experienced difficulties with a new chief constable who overturned the previous incumbent's policy of leaving indoor prostitution alone so long as no complaints were received by the police from neighbors. The brothel owner approached the GMB for help over this issue. She had previously been involved in some prostitute organizing attempts but had rejected approaching the ECP as she believed it to be too militant and political. The significance of this example was to be found in the partnership of owner and sex workers as well as in the IUSW floating the idea of 'unionized brothels' as a method to reduce exploitation and violence and running operations as a unionized workers' cooperative.

Representation and Campaigning Work

The GMB has represented and advised members in grievances against and disciplinaries from employers, as well as in dealing with the police and crown prosecution service. Examples of the former include successful claims of unfair dismissal for pregnancy against a club in 2002 and of unfair dismissal of a sex chatline operator in 2006, while instances of the latter concern securing justice through prosecution for rape of a prostitute in 2003, appealing against the awarding of Anti-Social Behavior Orders (ASBOs) against prostitutes, and opposing the shutting down of a Soho brothel and sex shop as a result of a compulsory purchase order in 2004. The GMB (and IUSW) has also carried out campaigning work against eviction of prostitutes from their rented flats by landlords and banning of the related use of business cards in public phone boxes to advertise their services. Under a 'servicing' rather than 'organizing' approach, the GMB helped offer lapdance training to prostitutes who wished to leave prostitution as a way of achieving this, as well as to existing lapdancers who wished to improve their skills; created a tax service for exotic dancers and prostitutes because these groups have experienced problems in gaining financial services because their earnings are cash-in-hand; and provided self-defence classes. One of the major tasks carried out by the GMB was to lobby the then-Labour governments (2001-2005, 2005-2010) in their review of the regulation of prostitution and sex work for decriminalization and the right of prostitutes to work together for their own safety and protection. This proved to be unsuccessful. However, the union did have more success in winning support for the sex work discourse within the wider union movement like the TUC and TUC Women's Conference (in 2003 but not 2009).

Conclusion

That most sex workers in Britain were shown not to be trafficked[49] means that most sex workers decide freely within the set bounds of a market system where and when to exchange their labor for money. Unlike unfree or bonded labor like slaves, this provides the basis for a union to collectively contest the conditions and terms of this exchange. For dancers, these issues concern stage fees, fines, shift patterns and overstaffing. Time will tell whether the GMB can build out of the bridgehead it has so far established, and become a player in the industry as it wishes; or whether it will be ensnared in the small outposts of a few independent clubs.

5

Other Countries in the Global North

This chapter examines sex worker unionization projects in the Netherlands, Germany, Canada, France and a number of other countries in the Global North. These various countries have differing forms of legal and moral regulation of the sex industry as well as different political and cultural complexions. Nonetheless, a common theme has been the attempt by sex workers to establish their own union organizations through self-agency for the purpose of interest representation and voice.

The Netherlands

In the Netherlands, the Red Thread was established in 1984 as a self-help group of prostitutes, based on the COYOTE pressure group model. It promoted recognition of prostitution as a legitimate occupation and pursued the interests of prostitutes by campaigning for rights and improvements in legislation, working conditions and welfare. However, the Red Thread began to move towards establishing a union in the late 1990s because it recognized unionization provided the best means of ameliorating poor working conditions and was an effective resource to gain decriminalization by (with decriminalization being necessary to allow a union to ameliorate poor working conditions). Before legalization, prostitutes employed by brothels, sex clubs and escort agencies were not entitled to claim unemployment benefit, sick leave, pensions or holiday pay because their places of work remained unlawful. Thus, following legalization in 2000, prostitutes involved in the Red Thread and who worked in brothels and sex clubs formed a union organization in 2002 called Vakwerk De Rode Draad (Red Thread union, RTu), to campaign for better pay and conditions because prostitution had now gained some legitimacy and was increasingly seen to be a normal 'profession'. The RTu received the help and support of the Federation of Netherlands Trade Unions (FNV), the largest trade union federation in the Netherlands, because the FNV had adopted a sex work discourse position.

The nature of the support given by the FNV has comprised office facilities, political access to the government, lobbying expertise, training for workplace reps and advice on negotiating collective agreements. However, recruiting was left solely to the RTu. At this time, the RTu was reluctant to campaign for employed status for prostitutes, fearing a loss of anonymity and control by them. However, as a result of prostitutes being obliged to pay tax, the realization on its part that employed status was necessary to avail prostitutes of certain rights, and the establishment by the FNV of a section for the self-employed, the RTu changed its position to accommodate to the need for employment contracts for employees. This facilitated a further series of meetings with the FNV where the RTu sought its support and help to gain access to its expertise and resources in terms of individual and collective bargaining, political clout, provision of training and increased legitimacy in society. In turn, this then led to several developments such as the creation of specific office facilities for unionizing prostitutes. The RTu, with the FNV, also attempted to create a form of industry-wide regulation by gaining the cooperation of brothel and club owners to agree to minimum standards in terms of sexual health as well as more conventional health and safety and working conditions issues. This proved unattainable because of employer opposition but with the legalization of brothels, brothels became workplaces subject to a new regulatory regime of licensing and inspection by local authorities for compliance with national labor laws (amongst other laws). Following the introduction of the new regime, many brothels either became illegal and unlicensed or went out of business because they would not submit to the minimum health and safety standards (e.g. fire, hygiene, safe sex, consensual sex, and personal security alarms) required for licenses.

That prostitutes have expressed concerns at the lack of change in their working conditions (e.g. rest breaks, long working hours, and holidays) since legalization has led to frustration with the RTu – even if this has been the result of the behavior of brothel owners. This is testament to the nature of the non-sex work social forces that largely determined the specific nature of the regime of legalization, and specifically the loss of anonymity and earnings (as a result of paying tax) when required to register as a sex worker. Consequently, only 10% of prostitutes are registered and, thus, eligible for social welfare benefits under legalization. So despite the FNV's help and support, the RTu has been slow to build its membership up even though subscriptions were set at a very low rate (of 40 Euros). There were around one hundred regular dues-paying members by 2004, rising a little before falling back and having more non-paying than paying members. The RTu hit financial problems in the mid 2000s because the Red Thread had its government funding cut and could not afford to subsidize it and the RTu never gained enough paying members – of between 3,000 and 5,000 – to fully join the FNV and gain access to its resources. These problems were compounded by the afore-mentioned closure of brothels and resistance to employed status.[50] Indeed, around a third of brothels and windows closed in Amsterdam in 2006 as the city withdrew licenses to target organized crime, with the impact of driving those affected prosti-tutes into illegal establishments in order to gain work. Although it still exists in a formal sense, the RTu no longer survives in much of a practical sense for it has ceased trying to pro-actively recruit and organize, and never established a website for this due to financial constraints. Yet, it retains a small number of key activists to offer advice and help to those that approach it.

Germany

Different city-based prostitutes' rights groups like HWG (Hookers United) have existed since the early 1980s. Prior to 2002, no union had shown any interest in organizing the 400,000-600,000 sex workers in Germany. However, the Unified Service Sector Union (Ver.di) began to organize and represent prostitutes in order to help improve their living and working conditions following a change in the legal status of prostitution in 2002 and after considerable internal debate on the costs and practicality of doing so. The change in legal regulation was similar to that of the Netherlands. Ver.di believed that prostitutes would require union organization and union help to avail themselves of the benefits of the legal change so created internal union structures for prostitute representation, developed dedicated standardized working contracts and established a legal advice service. Its first successes were in recruiting not insignificant numbers of prostitutes in Dortmund and setting up a works council in a Hamburg brothel. Following unionization, prostitutes in a number of brothels in Cologne threatened to go on strike in late 2003 against a proposal by the local authority to extend a 'pleasure tax' from casinos and amusement arcades to brothels, massage parlors, porn shows and table-dancing clubs.

However, these proved to be not much more than early flashes in the pan. So although Ver.di did not anticipate a rapid process of unionization, many prostitutes have been reluctant to take advantage of the new legal status of prostitutes as well as to join Ver.di for the same reasons found in the Netherlands, namely loss of anonymity and paying taxes. Indeed, by mid-2004, only one hundred prostitutes had joined, and they then rejected the proposed employment contract that Ver.di was to approach brothel owners with on their behalf because its weaknesses outweighed its strengths when taxed earnings were set against other benefits. Moreover, by early 2006, only 12% of prostitutes were registered.[51] This then has curtailed the number of potential union members very significantly. Nonetheless, a dozen collective contracts between prostitutes and brothel owners were signed.[52] Yet despite this, brothel owners continued to evade their employment responsibilities for paying social security contributions given the implications this has for their earnings. When a sex worker conference on organizing prostitutes in Germany in 2009 discussed the difficulties of doing so, it focussed upon the lack of social capital, poor educational levels, and paucity of stable and structured lives and communities as the main internal barriers to achieving external change in the context of the unfavorable nature of the regime of legal regulation. However, the view was that stigmatization played *the* major role in accounting for the ambivalence felt by prostitutes towards their own occupation. Thus, it was believed prostitutes internalize the stigma which helps convince them they are not engaged in an occupation that deserves social recognition, much less unionization. As a result, Ver.di has been forced – when circumstances allow – to merely proselytize for the benefits of unionization in order to try to convince prostitutes to join it. But it faces a 'Catch-22' situation, for without greater number of members it cannot establish the leverage over the salient issues with operators and local authorities it needs to in order to represent these sex workers.

Canada

Although labor unionism is far stronger in terms of density and influence on public policy in Canada than it is in the US, and Canada's labor law is more supportive of workers as well, the forces of sex workers' unionization are much weaker in Canada than in the US. Nonetheless, and based in Toronto, the Canadian Association of Burlesque Entertainers (CABE) was the first attempt to unionize sex workers. It was established in 1979 but disbanded in 1982. In its short life, it became Local 1689 of the Canadian Labour Congress (CLC) and was known as the 'strippers' union'. Its creation was spurred on by the closure of the Toronto office of the American Guild of Variety Artists (AGVA). In 1981, CABE applied to the Ontario Labor Relations Board in order to avail itself of the right to gain union recognition and, thus, conduct collective bargaining over terms and conditions of work of dancers at the Algonquin Tavern.[53] But in an echo of the situation found in the US,[54] the application was rejected as the dancers were deemed by the Board to be self-employed and not employees of the clubs. This was because the tavern management did not control the work of the dancers and the dancers had a high level of autonomy. CABE then sought the help of other unions such as Equity to develop its presence, but following such various difficulties CABE imploded.

The Association of Burlesque Entertainers (ABE) was formed in 1994 after a court decision to allow 'touching' in clubs. It argued against such unregulated lapdancing on the grounds of its similarity to prostitution, the health risks (from fingering, semen and vaginal fluids) and demeaning of the art of burlesque. Although ABE remained tiny and one of its main activists was dismissed, victimized and threatened for her union organizing attempts, it was successful in winning a subsequent ban on lapdancing and touching in 1995. Nonetheless, it was overwhelmed by the tide of pressure for touching and folded by the end of the 1990s. Earlier in Vancouver, the Vancouver Exotic Dancers' Alliance was established in 1981 and gained some 80 members very quickly. However, it was wracked by internal divisions and spent little of its time directly trying to represent dancers' interests.[55]

The Exotic Dancers' Alliance, a collective of current and former exotic dancers and their supporters, was established in 1995 in Ontario. Originally called the Exotic Entertainment Occupational Advisory Committee, the EDA sought to enable exotic dancers to promote their health, safety and well-being in a collaborative, collective and self-empowering manner and to work with government agencies, community groups, and interested business. It said of itself that it was dedicated to: 'building solidarity among exotic dancers; developing programs and services to improve the economic autonomy and well-being of dancers; and improving the treatment of dancers in the judicial system'. Campaigning for health insurance, better working conditions and employed status for dancers took place in many of the usual ways but also through trying to work with Adult Entertainment Association of Canada of club owners in the Greater Toronto area where some of the members of this association wished to establish self-regulation to develop minimum standards of employment. However, the EDA hit problems when one of its activists left to form the rival Exotic Dancers' Association of Canada (EDAC) in 2001, following personal and political differences. This may have evolved around EDAC willingness to work more cooperatively with employers/operators, since its membership was open to dancers, ex-dancers, supporters, pressure groups and businesses. At the same time, the Dancers' Equal Rights Association of Ottawa was created. With both the EDA and EDAC plowing the same furrow of campaigning for the dignity, health and safety and labor rights of dancers through dancer and public education, industry self-regulation, and public authority regulation, it was no great surprise that both become moribund by late 2004.[56]

The Strippers United Association was launched in 2004 to try to fill the vacuum but did not, being essentially stillborn. Into this gap, the Canadian Guild for Erotic Labour was founded in 2004 to promote labor rights and labor organizing workers engaged in erotic labor. But in recognition of previous difficulties of establishing new unions, it sought to convince other unions to help it organize sex workers (prostitutes and exotic dancers). Although it met with some success in doing so with the Canadian Union of Public Employees (CUPE) and the CLC, the results of this have not led to unionization itself. For example, the CUPE made clear its intention to support, rather than lead or facilitate, sex worker unionization and both the CUPE and CLC were equally supportive of public policy and regulatory change regarding the decriminalization of sex work. In the CUPE, opposition from the Women's Committee, as also in the case of the Confederation of National Workers' union, CSN, was important in preventing any implementation of supportive policy positions. The CUPE and CLC stance was essentially to take the same position as both the SEIU (in Canada) and the Canadian Auto Workers' (CAW)[57] union from 2005. This was to recognize sex workers as warranting a certification drive but not carry out any organizing work to achieve this.

Several other attempts at unionization in Canada were reported to have been made. One was in Ottawa when twenty sex workers met to discuss labor issues.[58] However, the meeting was not to establish a union but a sex workers' rights group which became POWER (Prostitutes of Ottawa-Gatineau Work Educate & Resist). POWER believes decriminalization of sex work is the key goal to be achieved, and thereafter the issue of unionization may be set in train. Another was in Winnipeg in mid-2009[59] but the outcome is not known, while the founding of Stripper Canada: A Community for Canadian Strippers replicated the passive non-union forms of collective organization in the US. Such an organization as POWER is far more common in Canada, highlighting that most of the collective organizations for sex workers are for prostitutes and take the form of advocacy and pressure groups (like the Sex Workers Alliance of Toronto (SWAT)). Most are city-by-city based although the Canadian Organization for the Rights of Prostitutes (CORP) – which was founded in 1983 and became the Sex Professionals of Canada in 2004 – has a more national presence. Given the difficulties faced in unionization of prostitutes, the British Columbia Coalition of Experiential Women (BCCEW) was established in 2005 and began to explore the idea of establishing a sex worker cooperative in Vancouver. As a result the West Coast Cooperative of Sex Industry Professionals was founded in 2007 and began work in 2008 on raising capital and developing business skills. The idea behind the cooperative was to create decent labor standards to improve the occupational health, safety and capacities of sex industry professionals as employees and contractors and do so within a legitimized profession. However, the inability to gain a change in the law so that a (legal) brothel could be lawfully established (as is the case in New Zealand or the Netherlands) as well as difficulties in raising sufficient capital have meant that the project has not yet come to fruition.

France

In many ways ironic given the occupation of churches in 1975 by prostitutes, it was not until 2009 that a union for sex workers – the Syndicat du Travail Sexuel (STRASS) - was founded in France. According to one of its founders, this was because of the weakness of unions in France in the private sector (with density of significantly less than 10%) and the dominant habits of direct action protest, as well as the strength of the abolitionist movement overall and radical feminism in the union movement. It took the re-emergence of a sex workers' protest in 2002 in response to proposals to criminalize certain acts surrounding prostitution to re-establish a sex worker movement in the country. The establishment of STRASS took several years of working within the Droits et Prostitution collective which was dominated by non-sex workers. STRASS initially gained 200 members which rose to around 500 by 2011 (out of an estimated 20,000 sex workers in France[60]). However, few members are openly active and not many are dancers or porn actors. Although explicitly formed as a union, one of the main activities it undertook was to resist the tightening of the regulation of prostitution (especially brothels) and the pressure for moves towards the Swedish model in 2011. In its wider work, STRASS has created good relations with health community organizations and is attempting to establish links with existing labor unions.

Other Continental European Countries

In 2007, a small group of sex workers in Turkey began moves to establish a union in order to protect the health, social wage and educational rights of sex workers, where the majority of them work without licenses (i.e. without being registered) and, thus, also social and welfare security.[61] One of the key tasks for the group was seen to be to reduce the discrimination and stigma that sex workers experience. The attempt to form the union was still ongoing in 2011 as a result of police harassment and brutality and murders of sex workers. These were designed to intimidate the activists from operating openly and publicly in order to reach other sex workers and challenge the discrimination and stigma. Undeterred, the activists organized the first 'red umbrella walk' in Ankara on International Sex Workers Day in 2011.

SALLI – the United Sex Professionals of Finland (literally, 'Union of Sex Business') was a union of sex workers in Finland founded in 2002 by nine sex workers. It called itself the 'union for all who work in erotic labor', namely, prostitutes, erotic dancers, dominatrixes, porn models and sex chatline workers. Its main aims were to address the problems sex workers faced in the domestic sex industry and provide health care information. Underlying these was the reality that it was more of a human rights organization than a labor union because it sought to promote sex workers' human rights in terms of their well-being, safety at work, professional skills, and control of workplace working conditions.[62] For example, it campaigned to allow prostitutes to work together without becoming liable to being criminalized for pimping. Between 2002 and 2006 it sought registration as an official association with the government and by 2005 had some forty members, of whom only half were sex workers, the remainder being supporters who were professionals like doctors and social workers. According to one of its founders in 2011: 'Sadly, SALLI does not exist anymore because there were not enough active members'. Whether this was because of the impact of the criminalization of the purchase of sex making sex work organizing more difficult is an open question.

The Hungarian Prostitutes' Interest Protection Association was founded in 2000 after prostitution was legalized in 1999, and in 2007 prostitutes were required to be registered as entrepreneurs. Although it was often referred to as a 'trade union'[63] and similar to SALLI, it is essentially an advice and support group, albeit one that has received substantial government funding to run programmes designed to promote the human rights of sex workers, to aid their social reintegration into society, and reduce their vulnerability. In Greece, the Movement of Greek Prostitutes is often called a both a 'union'[64] and an association, although it is more the latter as it is an advocacy and rights group. In Spain, there has been no attempt to form a union for sex workers despite the radicalism of some of the unions there and the call by one of the two main peak union federations for labor rights for prostitutes.[65] A number of activists in the CNT, the confederation of anarcho-syndicalist unions, contemplated forming one but were met by hostility and derision as a result of sex work not being seen as work, abolitionist views and male chauvinism.[66] In Eire, some lapdancers have made appeals to be unionized and two small unions entered into discussions with them on the possibility of union membership in 2003[67] while in Sweden some moves towards unionization and gaining union recognition were taken following legalization in 1999.[68] Nothing came of the talks in Eire, with the Sex Workers Alliance Ireland (SWAI) advocacy group being formed by current and former sex workers and their supporters in 2009 to promote the social inclusion, health, safety, civil rights, and the right to self-determination of sex workers. One of its tasks was to counter the campaign from 2011 to end prostitution called 'Turn off the Red Light' by establishing the 'Turn off the Blue Light' group to argue for decriminalization and positive images of sex workers in Ireland. Nothing appears to have come of the moves in Sweden.

IUSW's International Dimension

The sex worker activists and supporters who created the IUSW decided to name their organization neither the Union of Sex Workers nor the British Union of Sex Workers but the International Union of Sex Workers. This was for two reasons concerning the globalized nature of the sex industry. Although each country in the world has a domestic or indigenous sex industry, the problems and challenges are often common across borders, and sex workers frequently move between countries. However, the IUSW has sought not merely to reflect this globalization but also become an agency for the protection and advancement of sex workers' collective interests on an international basis albeit using the term 'international' was largely both an aspirational and symbolic form of solidarity with fellow sex workers.

Conclusion

In four countries – Netherlands, Germany, Canada and France – sex worker unions have been set up or sustained attempts to do so have been made. In other countries, the attempts have been far less certain, with many being wrongly heralded as union formations. Put together with the evidence of those in the US and Britain, a pattern emerges of the continual search by sex workers for effective collective interest representation. As the next chapter shows the same impulse can be found in a number of countries in the Global South.

6

Countries of the Global South

That the sex 'industry' is a globalized phenomenon is indicated *inter alia* by it being not confined just to the economies of the Global North. Therefore, this chapter looks at the attempts to organize sex workers in unions in the different national or domestic sex 'industries'. Even in the more developed economies of Australia and New Zealand, these almost all concern prostitutes rather than other types of sex workers.

Argentina

The Association of Women Prostitutes of Argentina (AMMAR) was formed in 1994 by some 60 sex workers and victims of violence inflicted by police. It grew to have some 15,000 members over the next ten years, particularly as it became a major organization in the national response to HIV/AIDS in Argentina. AMMAR took steps to transform itself into a union in 2001 with help from the CTA union confederation. Following this, the leader of AMMAR was shot dead in suspicious circumstances. Once part of the CTA, AMMAR instituted education reach-out programs and organized sexual health provision, and has gained changes in the legal regulation of prostitution in a number of cities. However, there is debate over whether AMMAR is a union of either sex workers or prostitutes or an association, that is, a rights group, of prostitutes.[69] This is because although AMMAR advocates labor and economic rights, it has not addressed the issue of the economic exchange between workers and operators (albeit in the context of the absence of employment contracts, employed status and fixed worksites). Yet it was reported in 2011 to be an unofficial union seeking official status as union and for sex work to be recognized as work.[70]

Elsewhere in South America, in 2007 prostitutes in Bolivia went on strike and refused to undertake mandatory STD testing to campaign against police harassment. The action was organized by ONAEM (National Organization for the Emancipation of Women in a State of Prostitution) which *Time* magazine called 'the sex workers' union'.[71] In Uruguay, a union of prostitutes is affiliated with the Central Workers' Union.[72] In Venezuela, a similar organization called Union of Men and Women Sex Workers and Associates (UNTRASEX) was founded in 1998 although it was denied the right to register as a legal union because the government considered that prostitution could not be defined as work as it lacked dignity and social justice, and legal unionization would lead to the expansion of prostitution.

Australia

The sex industry is Australia is often referred to as 'unionized'[73] and the Scarlet Alliance, the peak organization for sex worker rights groups, is often referred to as a 'union'. Both are inaccurate but not wholly so. Facilitated by moves towards both decriminalization and legalization, in 1995 the Prostitutes Collective of Victoria (PCV) and the Workers in Sex Employment (WISE) in the Australian Capital Territory (ACT) agreed to establish a union organization for prostitutes in alliance with the Liquor, Hospitality and Miscellaneous Workers' Union (LHMWU) despite some internal hostility from within the union. Both PCV and WISE had previously campaigned to improve prostitutes' working conditions in regard of fines for being late for work and dismissal for complaining about facilities. The PCV had approached others' unions but their responses were not encouraging given the prospect of the high cost involved in gaining small amounts of new members. The LHMWU's main work revolved around campaigning against grievances concerning non-payment of wages, payment of bonds, fines, charges for tea and coffee, long shifts, forced sex with owners and the right to demand condom usage. For example, prostitutes may spend all their shifts, of up to fourteen hours, without seeing a customer but be expected to clean, greet customers and do laundry for no payment.[74] This led to the demand for a basic wage. Moreover, the LHMWU sought to both improve conditions in individual brothels and lodge a sufficient number of wage and condition claims with individual employers to be able to gain a federal (bargaining) award covering, *inter alia*, sick pay, holiday pay, maternity, and pensions. Through its campaigning, the LHMWU achieved sick leave, some other leave entitlement, a minimum wage, security of employment and improved health and safety conditions in some brothels through a combination of legal action, collective bargaining, and working with some of the more progressive brothel owners. The union's other work has involved gaining representation on, and influence over, a number of government-funded health programmes for sex workers to ensure these are tailored to sex workers' needs as much as possible in terms of their objectives and methods of delivery (rather than being determined by public priorities).

While the normal challenges of loss of anonymity, paying full taxes and independent contractor status were found in Australia, one of the major reasons for the LHMWU's relatively limited advances was that it did not actively recruit individual sex workers, as well as its 'make or break' attitude. It worked through sex worker outreach organizations to reach potential members rather than direct recruitment, and stipulated that after an initial period of full resourcing if PCV and WISE could not deliver a certain level of membership to ensure self-sufficiency then the resource given would be reduced. As the level of membership was not delivered in this short period of time, the level of resource was then cut.[75] So although there technically remained coverage under an award until 2007, this was little used or implemented by the LHMWU.[76]

Amongst dancers, the Striptease Artists of Australia (SAA) was established in 2001 to provide representation to the 20,000 performers in striptease as no other union was attempting to do so. For example, in 1999 strippers in Queensland put out a public plea for unionization after being subject to fines for not turning up to work, for leaving early and for alleged violations of codes of conduct as well as the non-implementation of 'no-touching rules'. The response of the Media, Arts and Entertainment Alliance (MEAA) to look at the issues did not help resolve the dancers' concerns and the short-lived Queer and Esoteric Workers' Union of 1997 to 2001 was unable to improve matters. The SAA sought a federal (bargaining) award to set pay rates under which these sex workers would be classified as employees and not independent contractors who are charged stage fees to be able to work and, thus, ineligible for sick pay, occupational injury compensation and so on. In seeking the award, the SAA faced objections from four other unions including the LHMWU and MEAA over demarcations even though the four had not made any efforts to organize these workers. The differences were settled, allowing the SAA to register with the government for the consideration of an award in 2002 (with some 300 members at that point). Although the SAA sought constructive dialogue with employers, particularly to raise working standards across the sector, and spurned confrontation through strikes and picketing, the response from employers and operators was predominantly dismissive and hostile.[77] It took a further three years to gain an award. However, the dismantling of the federal award system along with vehement employer opposition meant that the award was not implemented and the SAA disintegrated under the pressure in 2007.[78] The formation of the Sex Workers' Union (SWU) in 2009 from within the Scarlett Alliance was a response to the failure of the LHMWU and SAA as well as the hope that the new replacement legislation (called FairWork) would help resuscitate the federal award system. Although the SWU attempted to use the new legislation, it was unsuccessful, and without much support from the Scarlett Alliance itself, the SWU remains more of an idea than a living entity.

India

In India, there are two unions for sex workers (mainly prostitutes).[79] One is in Karnataka, called the Karnataka Sex Workers Union (KSWU). It states it is a 'trade union of women, men and transgender sex workers, who live in the state of Karnataka. The Union seeks to be registered as a trade union in India. We advocate for the rights of all sex workers. ... We organize all persons who are working or have worked as sex workers in Karnataka. We strive to secure for them fair treatment and humane working conditions that will promote their living conditions and well-being. And we do this only through democratic, legitimate and constitutional methods. We plan to take care of our members through sickness, unemployment, old age, accident, and death'.[80] In 2006, it affiliated to the New Trade Union Initiative from 2006, a national federation of independent trade unions in India. So while the KSWU is explicitly a union and rejected the alternative of being an advocacy and rights group in order to be a *bona fide* organizer of sex workers to empower themselves as workers, rather than a provider of services to sex workers, this remains more of an aspiration in as much as there is no evidence of collective bargaining and workplace unionism. Instead, the KWSU has acted in a way similar to other sex worker unions in campaigning for decriminalization and better labor standards through public policy and legal reform. The Durbar Mahila Samanwaya Committee (DMSC or Durbar)[81] is the other reputed union, being established in 1995 and claiming to represent some 65,000 sex workers in West Bengal. As a community forum, credit cooperative, campaigning group and provider of sexual health services, it is not a union.[82]

However, Durbar did establish the Binodini Srameek Union (Entertainers' Labor Union) in 2002.[83] It was described as 'a putative trade union of sex workers, whose registration as a union has been applied for'.[84] Meanwhile, a union for *de facto* bar prostitutes was reported to have been established in 2004.[85]

New Zealand

Sex worker self-organization in New Zealand began considerably later than elsewhere, with the establishment of the New Zealand Prostitutes' Collective (NZPC) in 1987. It acts a prostitutes' rights group and not an 'unofficial union'[86] for sex workers as some believe. Despite a report of the New Zealand government's Occupational Safety and Health Service/Department of Labour[87] in 2004 highlighting that there was no single union in New Zealand that represents the interests of all sex workers and that some unions were seeking to have sex workers join, the only tangible sign of sex worker unionizing has come from the Unite union after the *Prostitution Reform Act* came into force in 2003 despite supportive noises from the New Zealand Council of Trade Unions for decriminalization. After the Service and Food Workers' Union was relaunched in 2003 as Unite – the union dedicated to organizing casual and low paid workers in the service, retail, hospitality, tourist and entertainment industries – it became, by default, receptive to organizing sex workers. Thus, some prostitutes and lapdancers, whether of employed or self-employed status, joined Unite and it indicated it was happy to support the creation of a union for sex workers. However, while prostitutes and lapdancers continued to join in small numbers, Unite has made no specific effort to organize them or establish a dedicated section of its union for them. This orientation changed in 2004 when Unite began to recruit telephone sex chatline workers and massage parlor prostitutes. By the end of 2004, it had membership amongst fifty sex workers and had represented about ten prostitutes in disputes with brothels. However, UNITE has found such organizing difficult because despite the signing of employment contracts, most sex workers are self-employed private contractors working within brothels, the NZPC advises that aggrieved sex workers have the option of industrial tribunals as well as unionization, and the *Prostitution Reform Act* has led to improvements in working conditions with regard to fining, right of refusing clients, coercion and health and safety. Thus, to date, Unite has one recognition agreement for collective bargaining over terms and conditions with the only known sex chatline operator and it continues to work with the NZPC, providing help for individual representation cases. Unite also had discussions with a number of dancers to establish their own 'exotic dancers' union' but the interest amongst the key activists waxed and waned so that nothing came of this.

South Africa

There have been several attempts to establish sex worker unions in South Africa. In the early 1990s, a street-walkers' association in Durban was begun but failed quite quickly. Then, in 1995, the Self-Employed Women's Union (SEWU) decided to organize commercial sex workers.[88] But by 1997 no progress had been made and it was decided that organizers should abandon this area of work. Failure to organize this group was likely to have been because of a strong commitment to Christian values from SEWU's leadership and staff. The key issue of the legality of prostitution and sex workers' employment status was highlighted by a case in 2007 when a sex worker challenged her dismissal from a massage parlor (brothel) by seeking the intervention of the Commission for Conciliation, Mediation and Arbitration. It, and then the Labour Court in 2008, ruled that prostitutes do not have rights under the country's constitution – not because of being of an employed status or not – but because the court could not be considered to sanction or encourage unlawful activity under the *Sexual Offences Act*. An earlier attempt in 2002 to strike down the Act relating to prostitution failed.

Nevertheless, the advocacy and rights group the Sex Workers' Education and Advisory Taskforce (SWEAT), based in Cape Town, has begun to make strides in garnering together the forces for conducting unionization of sex workers. SWEAT has long advocated that COSATU (Congress of South African Trade Unions) affiliate, the South Africa Commercial, Catering and Allied Workers Union (SACCAWU) should organize sex workers and established a close and positive relationship with it, leading SACCAWU to adopt a position of organizing sex workers in 2008. Yet, and in echoes of the situation found in both the SEWU and in Canada, unionization of sex workers by SACCAWU has yet to take place as a result of internal opposition to developing the tools to do so. However, SWEAT also helped launch the National Sisonke Sex Worker Movement of South Africa ('sisonke' meaning 'togetherness') in 2003 as another way of working for sex workers. Sisonke agreed its objectives were to unite to change laws with regard to sex work and get sex work recognized as work. Nonetheless, SWEAT continued to lobby for existing unions to undertake unionization of sex workers. As part of this it persuaded COSATU to adopt a sex work position and support calls for decriminalization[89] although when the issue came to COSATU's tenth national congress, the issue was referred back to the national executive as delegates were split on the issue. Thus, little progress has since been made (although the South Africa Police Union has also supported the sex work position and calls for decriminalization).

Conclusion

Other attempts to both found sex worker unions and to unionize sex workers are to be found in South Korea, China and Taiwan.[90]

For example, in South Korea, the National Female Workers' Association began organizing prostitutes into a union-type organization in 2005. Out of this emerged a putative union called the Democratic Coalition of Sex Workers (DCSW), which with over two hundred members in Kyonggi province, reached a collective bargaining agreement with brothel owners. However because prostitution is unlawful, the agreement had no legal binding. The Hanteoh Women Workers' Federation also organizes brothel prostitutes. But the furthest advances have been made in Australia as a result of the sex work discourse being embedded there since the 1970s and the existence of a federal system of collective arbitration which allows unions to gain industrial awards (essentially, industry-wide collective bargaining agreements). However, the arbitration system (which resulted in the awards) has effectively been abolished so that this advance has been turned back. Overall, the lack of progress in the most favorable environments, namely, Australia and New Zealand, indicates that as with the last chapter in regard of Germany and the Netherlands either legalization of prostitution *per se* is an insufficient basis for unionization of sex workers or that the particular complexion and nature of the regime of legalization is critical. Reflective of this, sex worker activists call rather for decriminalization.

7

Propensities and Obstacles to Unionization

The previous chapters recounted the particular ups and downs in the various projects and attempts to unionize sex workers and create sex worker unions. Despite some frailty and failure, and despite affecting limited numbers of sex workers so far, these attempts have provided voice mechanisms when none existed before. This has been through the creation of organs of self-agency (as opposed to paternalist and sometimes rather authoritarian third-party representation which concentrated on civil, political and human rights) as a result of movement to the discourse of worker/labor/economic rights. But voice has also led to changed and beneficial material circumstances relating to both state and employer/operator regulation. This chapter examines the more generalized forces and processes towards unionization of sex workers as well as those that impede unionization. This is done first by asking 'Why have sex workers become open to union organizing?' and 'Why have unions become open to organizing sex workers?'

Sex Workers Become Workers

To talk of sex workers means that a significant number, albeit still a small minority, of what can be objectively termed 'sex workers', whether prostitutes, dancers or porn actresses, have gone through a process of self-identification which has led them to conceptually categorize themselves as sex workers. Moreover, to perceive the act of providing sex, sexual services and sexual artefacts as comprising work provides a conceptual and moral legitimacy and normalcy to sex work on a par with other forms of work. Consequently, and notwithstanding any practical problems, this form of paid labor or work is now as open to unionization as any other should the required grievances emerge. To put the point another way round, the vast majority of workers, when contemplating forms of interest representation and unionization, do not have an *a priori* hurdle to straddle: they are workers and see themselves as workers. Whether they do then go on to form unions and unionize involves another set of issues and processes.

The ways in which these aspects of the sex work discourse have spread and the way in which self-identification has taken place have been important. It was not merely the case that the sex workers discovered the discourse from elsewhere external to themselves or that they were convinced of it by a body external to themselves. Rather, sex worker activists were themselves the major component of the social forces and processes by which the discourse of sex work (and sex workers) were created, refined and disseminated. This resulted from a protracted period of internal argument and then debate with external forces, whether sympathetic or hostile. The sex worker activists which did so were obviously the vanguard amongst sex workers in terms of their subjective consciousness. However, they have helped establish in an *objective* manner within academia and social science and, thus, wider society, the validity of the discourse.

The discourse's development and dissemination has been necessary – but on its own insufficient – to lead to the first steps towards unionization because it creates social legitimacy of sex work and for sex workers. Becoming a 'sex worker' signifies that this self-ascribed category of people are likely to perceive that they have interests which are different, separate and possibly in conflict with the interests of other groups within the sex industry, primarily, the owners, operators and employers. Moreover, it follows that individual sex workers are not sufficiently powerful on their own to prosecute their interests in contra-distinction to the owners, operators and employers so that banding together collectively becomes logical. Therefore, in conceptual terms at least there is a rationale, if not need, for the collective representation of the interests of sex workers. But representation of interests need not necessarily take the form of union representation as previous chapters have highlighted by virtue of the existence of advocacy and rights groups or other collective means like cooperatives. However, it has been the belief that labor unionism, notwithstanding current weaknesses and problems, offers a better way forward than these other means. This is because it is a more robust and grounded form of collectivism which seeks to deploy the collective power of workers at the worksite to further economic interests. The other side to this is recognition of the inadequacy of civil, political and human rights on their own as means to gain desired objectives alongside recognition of the inadequacy of the advocacy and rights groups of sex workers. Joining the broader union movement has availed sex workers of the legitimacy of being part of a social movement which has (in part) supported and vindicated the sex work discourse. However, the enjoining has also led to greater political influence to obtain the social wage and influence the nature of the regimes that regulate sex work. Of course, sometimes sex workers have had to create their own unions in the face of disinterest, hostility and ridicule from existing unions. This is a double testament to the strength of the activists' belief in the potency of labor unionism because establishing the structures of a union at the same time as recruiting and organizing sex workers is a Herculean task. That said, it is clear that sex worker unionization is a work-in-progress for on any number of issues its full potential has yet to be realized.

Unions Become More Open to Organizing Sex Workers

As previous chapters have recounted, the response from many existing unions to approaches from sex workers for membership has ranged from hostility to ridicule. Reasons for this include the stigmatization of sex work and sex workers, male chauvinism and sexism, male dominance within labor unionism and the strength of radical feminism that views sex work as exploitation and oppression of women as women.[91] It was not surprising then that sex workers have often created their own union organizations. However, this response of hostility to ridicule has not been a uniform one as individual unions in Australia, Britain, Germany, the Netherlands, New Zealand and the US have responded far more positively and union federations elsewhere have been supportive in other ways. There are a number of reasons for this over and above seeking new members and influence as well as in the newer and growing sectors of the economy like the private service sector.

First, sex workers – as a group wider than just prostitutes – have shown willingness to collectivize themselves in sufficient measure that raising the issue of unionizing sex workers has now arisen more concretely in the union movement. In practical terms, this has meant that unionizing sex workers could not be so easily dismissed by those inside the union movement who often relied on the argument that the workers themselves had to show some willingness to collectivize, unionize or organize themselves in order to receive help from unions to further do so. This evidence of self-organization has undercut to some extent reservations about helping to organize workers whose employment relationship was problematic for organizing, i.e. being variously self-employed, of independent contractor status, and operating in the 'black market' of not paying Income Tax or National Insurance.

Second, the influence of the radical feminist discourse amongst labor unions began to wane at the same time as the sex work discourse began to gain a small foothold. Given that unions believe in workers' rights and seek to organize as many workers as possible, it became a relatively small step for some to advocate the unionization of sex workers once they, and what they do, had been denoted as 'workers' and 'work'. Third, the sex industry has become relatively more respectable and tolerated in recent years as it has moved into the mainstream of economic activity and society. On the one hand, it has, or certain sections of it have, become less affected by criminal activity and more perceived as legitimate businesses. On the other hand, sexual mores have changed to some degree where sex and sexuality are more prominent and less inhibited within society. Fourth, the decriminalization and greater legitimacy of sex work by virtue of developments in state regulation have removed some of the reasons why unions were previously unwilling to respond positively to requests for unionization. Unions can now conceive of their role as one of representation of sex workers *vis-à-vis* public authorities and *bona fide* employers in a way similar to that of representation of other non-sex workers. Lastly, there has been, on the one hand, the emergence of the form of social movement unionism by which unions no longer fixate solely on the workplace as the locus of organizing and target of pressure. On the other hand, there has been the growth of the 'organizing approach' which is orientated around mobilizing over worksite grievances (rather than passively servicing members from outside their workplaces). Both have helped unions see that they could organize sex workers if they wished to.

Meeting of Minds

In the coming together of unions and the unionization of sex workers, a number of similarities are apparent. These concern the liberty of wage labor whereby workers seek fairness, justice and respect; the impulse to try to exert control over the labor market; the predominance of antagonism of interests with owners/ employers/operators and a greater preponderance to common or compatible interests with other workers; activists constituting a small cog that tries to turn larger ones, namely, members and potential members; and the struggle to transform passive membership into an active one. The latter struggle is typified by the contrast of 'organizing' versus 'servicing' approaches (where in the former members are collectively 'the union' and in the latter where individual members essentially buy protection as a form on insurance).

However, there are also some other obvious similarities. Both unions and sex worker union activists have sought to develop a form of unionism that is appropriate for transient workforces who work in a multiplicity of small and changing work locations. Recalling the GMB 'organizing the industry' approach in Britain, sex worker unions (new or existing) have adopted the approach of trying to establish favorable regimes of industry regulation, particularly because the sex industry is more subject to state regulation than most others. By attempting to engage employers and their business associations, political parties, and governments in political exchange (which is sometimes known as tripartite social dialogue), sex worker unions have sought to square the circle of creating influence over the determination of workplace conditions of employment in the sex industry whilst having little in the way of worksite presence, influence and rights. This approach comprises two main components. On the one hand, creating regulatory regimes (statutory, voluntary, semi-voluntary) in themselves that determine workplace governance from positions outside the worksite whilst, on the other hand, creating such regulatory regimes that allow or facilitate unionization. Here, the thorny issue of relationships with employers and government is broached in regard of cooperating whilst avoiding incorporation and loss of independence.

Barriers and Obstacles

The second half of this chapter now turns to barriers and obstacles towards unionization for it is apparent that the economic, legal, political and social conditions for creating and sustaining sex worker labor unionism remain uniformly difficult and challenging. Consequently, sex worker unions have often been forced to act as political pressure groups rather than as labor unions at the worksite as they hoped and intended. This has been particularly so because of the heavily regulated nature of sex work which either reinforces or maintains the stigma attached to sex work. Indeed, political-cum-public policy and legal reform are required not just to create lawful work but also a sense of social legitimacy. This provides the major reason why the sex worker unions have acted in a similar manner to the advocacy groups. The rider to this has been that legalization of prostitution in Australia, Germany, the Netherlands and New Zealand has not been the boon to sex worker labor unionism that was anticipated because sex worker groups did not have the upper hand in deciding upon the form of legalization. Rather, they were for decriminalization. But behind this are a number of important factors – or barriers and obstacles – that explain the limited progress to date. The consideration of these forms the remainder of this chapter.

Sex Work Discourse

The still limited presence of the discourse amongst sex workers – as well as within wider society – is the critical factor here because many others flow from it. Knowledge of, if not concurrence with, the discourse is likely to be a necessary – if not sufficient – prerequisite for unionization. Awareness and agreement provide the ideological and attitudinal resources to help generate a willingness to establish, join, and be active within a union. At the most, the discourse helps lessen the individually internalized ways in which sex workers experience stigmatization and helps increase their degree of self-confidence through legitimization. Most pertinently, sex workers would less fear the consequences of loss of anonymity if there was wider concurrence in society with the discourse. Indeed, the discourse provides for a certain degree of pride in being a sex worker that provides positive occupational identity. And from this, a sense of occupational identity would provide a solid foundation for attempts by sex workers to really make theirs the 'oldest *profession*'.[92]

However, part of the discourse is also potentially antagonistic towards the need for, and rationale of, unionization because there is a stress not only on legitimacy, skills and social usefulness, but that sex work is also financially rewarding and allows individual self-determination and control. Considerable significance is attached to relatively good pay for short working hours and the flexibility of working time, compared to routine jobs which are poorly paid and monotonous like waitressing and shop or bar work.[93] In other words, it can be rewarding labor and individual sex workers have, thus, little need of labor unions. The crux of the matter comes down to what the existing levels of these features are and whether and how they can be heightened. Much of this relates to individual sex workers' consciousness and their material circumstances of where they are in the hierarchy of the sex work labor market. Indeed, some sex workers that reject labor unionism for themselves – because of their superior material and labor market position – see it as necessary for other sex workers.

Paucity of Sex Worker Union Activists

Given that sex worker unions are historically embryonic and nascent, a key aspect for their development and growth (much less survival) concerns the number of activists they have to call upon to carry out their work and tasks. All were started off by small numbers – of less than ten key activists in most cases – and despite some of the sex worker unions having been in existence for a number of years, they have not been able to move beyond being reliant upon – indeed, often comprising – a tiny number of hyper-activists. The reason for collapse and disintegration of many sex worker unions has been that – notwithstanding what was meted out to them by employers/operators and the like – they were dependent upon such small numbers of activists, and when they experienced burnout or political decapitation the organization was itself killed off. The key point here is that the consequence of this is not just the continued reliance of sex worker union organization on a small handful of hyper-activists to sustain activity and representation but their inability to replenish their own stock. Overall, this paucity curtails organizing capacity and predisposes union organization to fragility.

From Campaigning to Representation

In addition to the difficulties in establishing unions in a period of reduced citizen participation in civil society and general retreat for labor unionism, and much more so for sex worker labor unions, many sex worker union organizations have also found making the transition from creation to existence and sustenance problematic. After the initial phase of organizing to create and launch a union, activists have often become tired and jaded, leading to smaller milieus of continuing activists. The process commonly begins with high levels of energy, vigor and excitement as a result of being involved in creating a new organization which has a specific objective and definite endpoint (i.e. of getting up and running). Euphoria greets creation. But once this point had passed, the organizations have a greater number of multifarious objectives which, in themselves, have no end points or finality as such. Moreover, sustaining organization becomes a quasi-separate, often burdensome, activity from implementing the organization's objectives, even though it essential for doing so.

The desire and pressure to maintain organization as the basis for trying to gain the objectives also leads small numbers of activists to substitute themselves for a wider number of activists, leading the former to become hyper-activists operating in a centralized manner. In the process, routinization as normalcy supersedes innovation and enthusiasm, and momentum is lost.

This overall process leads to internal tensions as frustrations – consequent upon the mismatch of resources and goals – are played out through individual and surface issues. Tensions are also involved in making the transition from just being a campaigning organization to one which carries out representative functions. These two functions have different rhythms and dynamics, with the former emphasizing membership participation and the latter de-emphasizing this as a result of officer specialization to carry out the representation. Indeed, the paucity of activists strengthens the push to service existing members, rather than organize to expand membership, and further concentrates activity amongst the lay officer cadre.

Labor Market Forces

The faster expanding supply within sex work labor markets relative to the (albeit also growing) demand for sex work is a significant factor here. Within this, sex work has become deskilled in as much as it is no longer the preserve of a small, 'deviant' and socially skilled minority. This is most obvious in the case of the transformation of striptease through the decline of burlesque and the rise of lap- and pole dancing. The size of the labor markets in exotic dancing and prostitution have both experienced growth – the former as a result of changing social attitudes where less stigma is attached to lapdancing, and the latter as a result of migration from the new EU accession states and countries of the former Eastern Bloc.[94] Cumulatively, sex work labor markets would then conventionally be termed 'slack', with little evidence of 'tight' sex work labor markets, so sex workers have seldom been able to benefit in the way other workers have been able to by taking advantage of the greater demand for, than supply of, labor. The problem for sex worker labor unionism here is that it, like labor unionism *per se*, is based on reducing levels of competition between workers within a trade or sector while at the same time trying to increase the price of labor by acting in a monopolistic manner. Where supply has outstripped demand, sex workers – like other workers – have been willing to undercut each other to get work and, thus, an income. This way lies the so-called 'race to the bottom'.

Social and Market Hierarchy

There is a profound sense of a social hierarchy amongst sex workers.[95] This manifests itself within sex workers *per se* and within sex worker sub-groups. At the bottom of the 'pile' for sex workers *per se* are street prostitutes while in the middle are sex chatline workers and towards the top are high-class 'call girls', well-known porn models, exotic dancers and porn stars. These classifications by sex workers are based on their values primarily concerning working conditions like safety, length of hours of work and sex worker choice of customers, earning capacity, and social status. The proximity to the sale of sex is often a key notion in these values. Closer proximity without what are regarded as considerable rewards is seen as undesirable. Distance from the sale of sex even without considerable rewards is still regarded as being preferable. Within prostitution, again street prostitutes are at the bottom with flat and brothel prostitutes above them and escort and 'call girls' at the top. Within other sub-groups, status is attached to earning ability, celebrity and popularity. For example, amongst exotic dancers there are several groups, with 'house dancers' being at the bottom along with the touring 'road girls', then 'freelancers' further up while at the top are the 'feature dancers' who are minor starlets and personalities within the sector. The salience of this is that the union maxims of 'unity is strength' and 'an injury to one is an injury to all' have far less purchase when divisions and difference are more prominent. Moreover, this makes it harder to identify the sense and forums of sex worker community or occupation where similarities outweigh differences.

Self-Employment and Market Proximity

The predominance of self-employment in the sex industry is antithetical to the traditional, semi-permanent bilateral relationship between worker and employer upon which labor unionism conventionally depends. Often this means there is no obvious bargaining 'partner' to deal with. That sex workers as individuals also deal directly with their contractors, whether these be 'service providers' (e.g. porn makers or stripclub owners) or the actual end-users (e.g. customers of prostitutes), personally negotiating the terms of the exchange is another instance of this antithesis. Yet, freelancer and self-employed workers are often unionized as the SAG and Equity show in the US and Britain respectively. Without wishing to underestimate the difficulties, it seems the issue is, thus, more about what type of unionism is effective and appropriate and not necessarily whether unionism *per se* is appropriate.

Other Factors

There are a host of other factors which help retard and impede unionization. Amongst these is the individualized nature of the sex work labor process and the relative absence of the 'collective laborer', defined as collectives of workers engaged in collectively producing a good or service as a result of the division of labor. Added to this is the small size of many sex work enterprises so that it seems that problems can be sorted out directly, and without the need of a third party. Moreover, a common disincentive to unionization is often the prevalence of non-union methods of interest representation such as the sex worker rights groups, 'ugly mugs' schemes, boycotting working at certain clubs and various individual-based personal coping and distancing mechanisms.[96] These factors make labor unionism seem irrelevant to many sex workers. Employer/operator hostility is another as the previous chapters have made clear. Finally, and perhaps to a surprising degree, sex worker unionization projects have attained some support from existing, mainstream labor movements. But there has still been a reticence to actively support and fully embrace them. To unionization projects which are fragile and embryonic, this has been all the more critical.

Conclusion

The progress, notwithstanding problems encountered and limited progress to date, in the unionization of sex workers mean that the claim of American university professor of women's studies Donna Hughes, that 'unionization of 'sex workers' is a leftist fantasy'[97] has no basis in fact. What is far more credible to suggest, having a basis in fact, is that the embryonic forms of sex worker unionization described and analyzed in this book *may* provide the platform from which further growth and development *may* occur.

8

Conclusion

Collective interest organization amongst sex workers is essential to counter-balance the power of customers, operators and state regulators. This is all the more so as operators have increasingly applied neoliberalism towards sex workers, namely, by making them self-employed contractors which are responsible for pay operators to work. In offloading costs and responsibilities without losing control, they have saddled sex workers with costs but no more control. Unionization is one of the, if not, *the* most potentially powerful means of providing collective self-interest organization for workers. Thus, labor unions provide the potential of not just exerting some control over the wage-labor bargain with owners and operators but also the means by which to do so. In other words, labor unions are founded on the principle of self-reliance facilitating self-control.

To date, projects to unionize sex workers have been slow, fitful and fragile despite many notable, heroic and continuing attempts. Even though their mere existence can be viewed as a triumph in itself, attempts in both the Global North and South have met significant problems, obstacles and challenges. Thus, no shining exemplar has yet been created to guide and inspire others to strength and success in the sex workers' quest for social, political and economic justice.

The attempts recounted and analyzed in this book could be looked at in one of three ways. First, they disintegrate and collapse or keep failing to make sufficient progress, suggesting that unionization is either inappropriate *per se* for sex workers or just in the practice of the particular time and place. It may be that more conducive regimes of regulation are needed for the promise of unionization for sex workers to be delivered upon. Decriminalization rather than legalization (involving registration) would be an obvious deduction here.

Or second, that, despite such failures, the underlying impulse for social justice in work keeps compelling sex workers to try again and again so that the issue is really about what is the most appropriate form of labor unionism for the particular circumstances of the sex industry. Such a view would easily fit into the mobilizing perspective from anger, to hope, to action, when applied to the world of paid work and wage labor. Here there is diagnosis and prognosis, whereby anger at a grievous situation leads to the hope that something can be done about this and this leads to people collectively taking action.

Or third, that these unions have been forced (back) into acting in a similar manner to their professed antithesis, namely the prostitutes' rights groups as a result of the loss of initial momentum. Thus, they have concentrated on political lobbying on public policy, projects of legal reform of sex work, and helping provide individualized assistance to sex workers inside and outside their worksites on health issues, criminal offences and business matters. Collective bargaining and collective representation at work over the terms of the wage-effort bargain, thus, have taken a back seat. In other words, the sex worker unions are not really unions.

But either way, it seems that the vanguard of sex workers themselves will not give up upon attempts to make their working lives better in the here and now through these union projects and initiatives. This is all the more so when they see that many of the problems encountered in sex work are due to legal and non-legal (like public morality) regimes of regulation rather than something inherent in sex work itself. The belief is that there is no reason why certain modes of control and regulation of exotic dancing, for example, cannot make the experience of the dancers better and that unions are needed to gain this and then monitor and enforce this.

Given this, the focus of attention shifts to the issue of what form of labor unionism is most appropriate and effective for sex workers. One based on an occupational identity would seem the most promising because it is the form most suited to dealing with sex workers either being self-employed or working alone or in small numbers in many small establishments. This type of unionism – through influence over the labor market and supply of labor – is able to establish and enforce minimum employment standards. The battle will be not only to counter the resistance to this form of regulation from employers and operators but to establish the sense of occupational identity and community that is needed to underpin this form of collective interest representation in the first place.

Endnotes

1. While sex workers may be seen as having a monopoly of specialist knowledge, expertise and skills, there are no signs that the case that they could then be termed sex therapists, sex surrogates or counsellors has had much traction.
2. To do otherwise, i.e., literally sell one's body, would be sell oneself into slavery.
3. The study of sex worker unionization up to late 2004 in Australia, Britain, Canada, Germany, Netherland, New Zealand and the US is explored in greater detail in Gall, G. (2006) *Sex Worker Union Organising – An International Study*, Palgrave. A condensed version of this study can be found in Gall, G. (2007) 'Sex worker unionization: an exploratory study of emerging collective organization' *Industrial Relations Journal*, 38/1, pp70-88 while studies of others aspects of sex worker collectivism can be found in Gall, G. (2009) 'Union organising with 'old' and 'new' industrial relations actors: the cases of sex workers in Australia and the United States' in Gall, G. (ed.) *The Future of Union Organising – Building for Tomorrow*, Palgrave, pp173-184, and Gall, G. (2010) 'Sex worker collective organization: between advocacy group and labor union?' *Equality, Diversity and Inclusion*, 29/3, pp289-304.
4. See Gall, G. (2006) *Sex Worker Union Organising*, pp46-64, for a longer consideration of these antecedents.
5. Tax, M. (1980) *The Rising of the Women – Feminist Solidarity and Class Conflict, 1880-1919*, Monthly Review Press, New York, pp21, 66, 69.
6. Foner, S. (1979) *Women and the American Labor Movement: From Colonial Times to the Eve of World War 1*, Free Press, New York, p421, and Hall, C. (1999) *Labor Struggles in the Deep South and Other Writings (edited and introduced by D. Roediger)*,

Charles H. Kerr, Chicago, p81.

7. Wilmet, H. (1999) 'Naked feminism: the unionization of the adult entertainment industry' *The American University Journal of Gender, Social Policy and the Law*, 7/3, p466, and Burana, L. (2001) *Strip City: A Stripper's Farewell Journey Across America*, Virago, London, p150.

8. Wilmet, H. (1999) 'Naked feminism', p466.

9. Cobble, D. (1991) *Dishing it Out: Waitresses and their Unions in the Twentieth Century*, University of Illinois Press, Urbana, pp128-129 and Cobble, D. (2010) 'More intimate unions' in Boris, E. and Salazar Parrenas, R. (eds.) *Intimate Labors*, Stanford University Press, Palo Alto, p290.

10. Cobble, D. (2004) *The Other Women's Movement – Workplace Justice and Social Rights in Modern America*, Princeton University Press, Princeton, pp2-3.

11. Ross, B. (2000) 'Bumping and Grinding On the Line: Making Nudity Pay' *Labour/Le Travail*, 46, pp221-50 and Ross, B. (2006) ''Troublemakers' in Tassels and G-Strings: striptease dancers and the union question in Vancouver, 1965–1980' *Canadian Review of Sociology*, 43/3, pp329-344.

12. Roberts, N. (1986) *The Front Line*, Grafton, London, pp89-90.

13. Gall, G. (2006) *Sex Worker Union Organising*, pp65-66.

14. See Gall, G. (2006) *Sex Worker Union Organising*, pp72-78, for an extended discussion.

15. Wilmet, H. (1999) 'Naked Feminism', p467.

16. Wilmet, H. (1999) 'Naked Feminism', p468.

17. Wilmet, H. (1999) 'Naked Feminism', p467.

18. *Philadelphia Weekly* 6 March 2002.

19. Ward, C. (2005) 'America's least trusted - how a Clermont stripper ended up under FBI surveillance' *creativeloafing.com*, 28 December.

20. *Washington Post* 15 March 2010.

21. *The Nation* 3 April 2003.

22. Gall, G. (2006) *Sex Worker Union Organising*, pp85-86.

23. 10 August 2005.

24. 29 January 2005.

25. Majic, S. (2005) 'Live! Nude! ... Organized Workers? Examining the organization of sex workers in Las Vegas, Nevada', Cornell University, Ithaca.

26. This problem had its parallel where an attempt to create a producers' association with a rate structure failed.

27. *In These Times* 18 October 2010.

28. *Whack! Magazine* 27 September 2011.

29. 'Porn History 101: How many porn performers does it take to start an association?' *Adult Cyber Mart*, 2011.

30. Leigh, C. (1987) 'The Continuing Saga of Scarlot Harlot IV' in Delacoste, F. and Alexander, P. (eds.) *Sex Work: Writings by Women in the Sex Industry*, Virago, London, p89.

31. MacCowan, L. (1997) 'Organising in the message parlor: an interview with Denise Turner' in Nagle, J. (ed.) *Whores and Other Feminists*, Routledge, New York, pp232-241.

32. *New York Post* 6 October 2008.

33. Jenness, V. (1993) *Making It Work: The Prostitutes' Rights Movement in Perspective*, De Gruyter, New York, p115.

34. Even in Nevada, where some brothels are legal, the sex workers there are not employed.

35. Although it can be observed that the creation of branch 690 based on 'trade' – thus, spurning its long held principle of industrial unionism – was a break for the IWW, it did signify recognition of the specificity of sex work and the marginalization of sex workers. However, the creation of branch 690 was an attempt to show political solidarity and to aid discussion rather than to actually organize workers.

36. *Williamette Week* 18 November 2009.

37. See American Rights at Work website (http://www.americanrightsatwork.org/).

38. However, *Labour Research* ('Can unions represent sex workers?' 2007, 96/3:23) quoted the president of the GMB sex

workers' branch as putting the figure at three hundred.

39. See her http://toomuchtosayformyself.com/2009/01/09/the-great-iusw-con/. The basis for this charge was that one prominent IUSW and GMB member was Douglas Fox who was a sex worker and owner of an escort agency. He encouraged his escorts to join the IUSW and GMB. Fox subsequently left the IUSW and GMB for reasons unknown. Another example was that the Tables Dancers' Union GMB section was the owner and manager of Club Crème.

40. *Guardian* 10 November 2011, 16 March 2002 respectively.

41. 'Can unions represent sex workers?' 2007, 96/3:23.

42. Although there is a legal right to accompaniment-cum-individual representation for union members under the *Employment Relations Act 1999*, this only applies to employees.

43. Another reason may be fairly high levels of job satisfaction - see Sanders, T. and Hardy, K. (2010) *Research on Lap Dancing in England: Preliminary Findings*, University of Leeds, Leeds.

44. This was why the Lapdancing Association (LDA) of operators was established in 2006 and represented a third of clubs and played a major role in attempting to moderate the change in the licensing system for clubs. The attempt to establish minimum standards was also to prevent under-cutting by the entry into the market of so-called 'cowboy' competitors.

45. The other reason for campaigning for keeping clubs open is to stop them going underground which endangers the dancers and increase stigmatization.

46. *Evening Standard* 18 November 2011, *Guardian* 19 November 2011.

47. *Independent on Sunday* 30 June 2002.

48. *Morning Star* 18 December 2003

49. Mai, N. (2011) *In Whose Name? Migration and Trafficking in the UK Sex Industry*, London Metropolitan University, London

(see also *Guardian* 20 October 2009, 19 August 2010). The same also appears to be the case in Eire (*Sunday Independent* 5 September 2010).

50. See Wijers, M. (2008) 'Prostitution policies in the Netherlands' La Strada International – the European Network against Trafficking in Human Beings, Amsterdam.
51. *Associated Press* 18 January 2006.
52. *Hamilton Spectator* 14 May 2005.
53. Couto, A. (2006) 'Clothing exotic dancers with collective bargaining rights' *Ottawa Law Review*, 38/1, p55.
54. The Canadian recognition law is based on that of the US so it is not surprising that it only pertains to employees as well.
55. Ross, B. (2006) ''Troublemakers' in Tassels and G-Strings'.
56. In fact, EDAC continued to exist but as a front for its president's business venture, LiveGirlProductions, rather than a dancers' organization.
57. Couto, A. (2006) 'Clothing exotic dancers with collective bargaining rights', p40. The CAW has begun in recent years to organize workers outside its traditional remit.
58. *Ottawa Citizen* 18 February 2008.
59. *See Magazine* 13 August 2009.
60. *Guardian* 13 April 2011.
61. *Hurriyet* 8 November 2008.
62. Therefore, it was erroneous for some like Ross, B. (''Troublemakers' in Tassels and G-Strings') to call it a union.
63. See, for example, *Global Post* 12 May 2010 or its Wikipedia entry.
64. See, for example, *Associated Press* 20 January 2010.
65. *BBC News Online* 18 May 2005.
66. Iniguez de Heredia, M. (2007) 'History and actuality of Anarcha-feminism: lessons from Spain' *Lilith: A Feminist History Journal*, 16, pp42-56.
67. *Irish Independent* 26 September 2003.
68. Clamen, J. and Lopes, A. (2003) 'Labour organizing in the

sex industry: The way forward? The IUSW experience'
Research For Sex Work, 6, p30.

69. See Hardy, K. (2008) http://katehardy.wordpress.com
/2008/07/18/despite-violence-and-marginalisation-sex-
workers-in-argentina-are-leading-the-way-on-hivaids-
prevention/, Hardy, K. (2010) 'Incorporating sex workers into
the Argentine labor movement' *International Labor and
Working Class History*, 77/1:89-108, and Reynaga, E. (2005)
'Violence against sex workers and the role of unions'
International Union Rights, 12/4:3-4.

70. *Metro* 29 November 2011.

71. 24 October 2007.

72. *Inter-Press Service* 11 February 1998.

73. See, for example, Walsh, J. (1996) 'The world's first prostitutes' union' *Marie Claire*, January, pp48-51.

74. For other ways in which the work of prostitutes is similar to
other forms of work in terms of how it is organized and
regulated by employers/operators see Sullivan, B. (2008)
'Working in the sex industry in Australia: the reorganisation
of sex work in Queensland in the wake of law reform' *Labour
& Industry*, 18/3, pp73-92. In the case of dancers, see Murray,
K. (2003) 'Labour regulation in the legal sex industry in
Victoria' *Australian Journal of Labour Law*, 16, pp321-342.

75. Murray, K. (2001) 'Sex Work as Work: Labour Regulation in
the Legal Sex Industry in Victoria' Master of Law Thesis,
University of Melbourne, Melbourne, pp227-228.
Furthermore, the Scarlett Alliance believed the biggest
barrier to unionization of sex workers in Australia is the
existing union movement and its 'whorephobia'.
Consequently, it see that unionization will take place, if it
takes place at all, through new unions being formed for sex
workers by sex workers.

76. The dismantling by a Conservative government of the
federal award system between 1996 and 2009, of course, did

not make this situation any easier.

77. Gall, G. (2006) *Sex Worker Union Organising*, pp131-132.

78. The abolition of the so-called 'WorkChoices' legislation and its replacement by the 'FairWork' legislation from 2009 has not reversed the situation sufficiently as to stimulate any sex worker union initiatives other than the SWU.

79. The Sex Workers Forum Kerala has wrongly been characterized as the Kerala Sex workers Union.

80. KSWU website 'Introduction' (http://sexworkersunion.in/?page_id=2).

81. The literal translation is the 'unstoppable women's synthesis committee'.

82. Thus, commentators like the *Press Trust of India* (17 February 2000), *Times of India* (18 March 2001), Gallin, D. (2003) 'Note on the International Sex Workers' Movement' (Global Labour Institute, Geneva), and Shah, S. (2003) 'Sex work in the global economy' *New Labor Forum*, 12/1:74-81 are wrong to do so.

83. Kotiswaran, P. (2011) *Dangerous Sex, Invisible Labor: Sex Work and the Law in India*, Princeton University Press, pp222, 238.

84. Bandyopadhyay, N. (2008) 'Streetwalkers Show the Way: Reframing the Global Debate on Trafficking from Sex Workers' Perspectives', Institute of Development Studies Working Paper 309, Brighton, p6.

85. *Business Line* 17 September 2004.

86. *Dominion Post* 20 September 1999.

87. OSHS/DoL (2004) *A Guide to Occupational Health and Safety in the New Zealand Sex Industry*, Occupational Safety and Health Service/Department of Labour, Wellington.

88. Devenish, A. and Skinner, C. (2004) 'Organising Workers in the Informal Economy: The Experience of the Self Employed Women's Union, 1994-2004', University of KwaZulu-Natal.

89. *Cape Times* 14 September 2009. It was also reported by this newspaper that unionization and decriminalization were

interim positions for 'Cosatu hopes sex work will die a natural death as 'the struggle for socialism to change social and economic conditions as well as mindsets will eliminate the excesses of sex work and in the long run eliminate (it) in our society'.'

90. See Gall, G. (2006) *Sex Worker Union Organising*, p154.

91. But some of the resistance also came from unions having a lack of knowledge and experience of operating in the sex industry – and were concerned about the costs and chances of success in doing so –making this a more pragmatic than political perspective.

92. See point made at outset of book in regard of the control that professions exert over their members. Yet there is a complexity here for selling sexual services straddles the divide between those that sell actual sex and those that do not. In practice, many sex workers like dancers, dominatrixes, sex chatline workers attach significance to this which creates a schism with those that do.

93. Another aspect here of the discourse is that some sex workers believe themselves to be entrepreneurs who are more concerned about their right to do business without interference from others than anything else.

94. The issue of forced and bonded labor through trafficking is salient here although it would appear that the extent of forced trafficking is commonly exaggerated. See, for example, Mai, N. (2011) *In Whose Name?*

95. See Weitzer, R. (2009) 'Sociology of sex work' *Annual Review of Sociology*, 35, pp213-234.

96. An obvious example of the latter is to create separate personas for work and non-work lives.

97. *National Review* 11 May 2004

Contemporary culture has eliminated both the concept of the public and the figure of the intellectual. Former public spaces – both physical and cultural – are now either derelict or colonized by advertising. A cretinous anti-intellectualism presides, cheerled by expensively educated hacks in the pay of multinational corporations who reassure their bored readers that there is no need to rouse themselves from their interpassive stupor. The informal censorship internalized and propagated by the cultural workers of late capitalism generates a banal conformity that the propaganda chiefs of Stalinism could only ever have dreamt of imposing. Zer0 Books knows that another kind of discourse – intellectual without being academic, popular without being populist – is not only possible: it is already flourishing, in the regions beyond the striplit malls of so-called mass media and the neurotically bureaucratic halls of the academy. Zer0 is committed to the idea of publishing as a making public of the intellectual. It is convinced that in the unthinking, blandly consensual culture in which we live, critical and engaged theoretical reflection is more important than ever before.